PRAYER, PRAISE
AND PANDEMIC

PRAYER, PRAISE AND PANDEMIC

A 60-Day Devotional for Responding in
Times of Crisis

David Crosby

Luke 1:30-33

IRON STREAM
B O O K S
An Imprint of Iron Stream Media
Birmingham, Alabama

Iron Stream Books
100 Missionary Ridge
Birmingham, AL 35242
An imprint of Iron Stream Media
IronStreamMedia.com

Iron Stream Media serves its authors as they express their views, which may not express the views of the publisher.

Library of Congress Cataloging-in-Publication Data [to be filed]

ISBN-13: 978-1-56309-463-7

Ebook ISBN: 978-1-56309-464-4

1 2 3 4 5—24 23 22 21 20

For the marvelous friends I grew to know and love through years of working together and praying for each other

Contents

Introduction

We are living through a strange and confusing season in our community, our country, and our world. We see the blush of light upon the horizon, but many are uncertain whether the light is waxing or waning, whether the sun is rising or setting.

We want this health crisis to be over yesterday, but it will not fade until some future tomorrow. Meanwhile, we are anxious about our health and wellbeing, about the future for ourselves and the ones we love, and for our personal finances. We are lamenting some past decisions and celebrating others.

These devotionals are intended to turn us toward the future that belongs to God. It is my small effort to increase our faith and to intensify our prayer life as individuals and as the church of Jesus Christ on mission in a rapidly changing world. We should not be anxious about tomorrow, even when it is the year 2020, the year of COVID-19. Jesus said that each day has enough trouble of its own. He urges us to enjoy the Father's peace no matter what comes as the world turns.

Jesus also taught us how to use stories to bring home spiritual truths. Most of the stories to follow are vignettes of my life as a father, a pastor, and the second born of thirteen children. I wrote them over a period of years and edited them for this devotional series. They are glimpses into my life and maybe into yours.

If you read the Scripture reference, the daily devotional will take approximately nine minutes to complete. I hope these stories will make you smile, give you hope, and help you get ready for whatever is coming.

Day 1

What a great day to begin a new commitment in prayer. I remember a Sunday morning, ages ago, when a missionary tapped me on the shoulder and asked me if I needed to pray. He could see the distress in a child's face.

I moved out of the wooden pew and made my way to the altar rail in our little church in Hawley, Minnesota. I knelt in prayer, asking God to direct my life and offered myself to Him however He wanted to use me. We used the prayer rail frequently in our church, and I was not conscious that other people were watching me—only God. I was intent on pleasing Him alone.

Reflecting now, I see that day as a significant part of my journey toward discovering God's purpose in my life. I cannot remember all the details of the moment, but I picture in my mind a young boy, hands folded, knees resting on a red cushion at the prayer rail, his feet protruding out upon the hardwood floor. I see his head bowed, and I hear his whispered prayer of petition: "Lord, show me what to do, and I will do it."

The heart of prayer is simply acknowledging God as Lord and offering ourselves to Him. Without such surrender, our words are only empty noises.

Recognize in prayer today that Jesus Christ is Lord of your life, and submit yourself to him. Then commit this season of the coronavirus to him. You do not know all the future holds, but God does. He did not need the morning news to get His update. He knows the end from the beginning. All that we worry about he has under complete control.

Scripture: Matthew 6:25–34

Prayer: *Oh God, let Your peace abound among the church and throughout our world in this season of crisis. Give us serenity in place of our anxiety and faith in place of our fear. Prepare my heart and our church for our assignment as Your people in this strange time.*

Day 2

My son, Joshua, and I went exploring with a church group on the Colorado River in Texas just above Lake Buchanan. We intended to fish, but the river was swollen by rains upstream. The fishing was terrible, but exploring was fun.

We watched a crane as he dove off a towering rock ledge and flapped and cruised his way upward in spiral flight. We caught a glimpse of a huge alligator gar looking for food along the bank of the muddy river. We saw ten thousand mud martins darting in and out of the cliffs.

And we spied a lone cactus, wedged in a slit on a sheer rock cliff, thirty feet from the ground, its deep red blossoms startling the eye on the face of that grim gray wall.

God did that. Only He could create such a seed, so hungry for life, able to sprout with a hint of soil, then send its tender roots into the crack, groping for moisture. Only God could make that cactus, suspended on the cliff, find a hold and produce a full bouquet of beautiful flowers.

Maybe you feel like a cactus grasping for footholds on the rock. Sometimes I feel that way. The world seems stern, maybe even cruel; times are hard. You are barely hanging on.

The Great Landscaper of the universe sets a splash of brilliant red amid the rocks, transforming the foreboding into the intriguing.

Watch him do this today with your virus-infected landscape.

Don't let the coronavirus dominate your mind and spirit. Think about the Lenten season. We rehearse each year during those days the passion of our Lord in that last week of His life on earth.

We see the response of Jesus amid the harsh stone, the great difficulty. Stripped and beaten, mocked and ridiculed,

He hung suspended on nails in front of a crowd. What will He do now, this holy man from Nazareth?

He will forgive His executioners. He will care for His mother. He will promise paradise to a thief. He will finish His work. Here we have a bouquet of blossoms on a sheer rock wall, the beauty of holiness hanging on a cross. We are startled by this man from Galilee. He hurls no insults, but through the mist of pain sees people in need and gives to them the baptism of His love.

Follow Jesus through the maze today. Your retirement fund is down 30 percent. You are worried about paying the bills. You are missing the usual gatherings.

Call your elderly neighbor. Make sure he or she has everything they need to navigate these difficult days. Check on the single parent next door. Find a way to bless somebody near you. Set the Father's brilliant love on display, like a bouquet on a grim gray wall.

Scripture: Hebrews 12:1–13

Prayer: *God, help me to "bloom where I am planted," displaying Your loving presence even through the trials of this unique and unexpected season. Give me courage to join You in the startling work of grace.*

Day 3

The steadfast love of the LORD never ceases; his mercies never come to an end; they are new every morning; great is your faithfulness. —Lamentations 3:22–23

Here, let me show you a picture. I took it yesterday. I was making the corner, going to get milk, when I saw this wobbly-legged newborn staggering around his mother. She had just delivered him.

My shepherd brother-in-law said, "Now you're a sheep farmer—the first lamb born on your property."

Jesus told the story of the lost sheep. The shepherd left the ninety-nine sheep in the fold and went searching for the one that was lost. When he found it, he put it on his shoulders and carried it home. He was so happy that he called all his friends for a party.

I struggled a little bit each time I read that parable, wondering why a grown man would be so happy to find a sheep that he would sling it on his shoulders for the long walk home from the field. But when I saw this little lamb I realized how precious and amazing these creatures are. I picked her up, the mother watching, and carried her to the stable.

The steadfast love of the Lord never ceases. His mercies are new every morning.

God is doing something new in you and for you. Receive this truth as you move through your day. Keep your eyes open for the mercies that God extends to you—moments of grace, beauty, and goodness that reveal His presence in your life.

Scripture: Psalm 23 (the Shepherd's Psalm)

Prayer: *Walk with me today, Lord Jesus. Help me to know Your presence. Help me to see Your mercies.*

Day 4

The ewe and her two-day-old lamb grazed the pasture yesterday. I released them from the pen because I have never seen a dog or coyote in that pasture.

Until yesterday when I got home. The minute you think they are safe something happens.

A dog as big as a small horse was in the little pasture with the sheep! When I shouted and started toward him he ran away terrified, forcing his long body through a hole in the field fencing.

Ewes are almost defenseless. They can bite, but not effectively. They can kick, but not very hard. A ram can knock you over with his head. I am a witness. But ewes and lambs are very vulnerable creatures.

Good shepherds take good care of their sheep. I am trying to discover how the dog got in the pasture. Maybe the same way he got out. And I am going to walk the perimeter with wire cutters and wire, closing up any holes that dog could get through.

I wrote a song for my children when they were preschoolers. The chorus goes:

I am a lamb, I am, I am
Jesus knows my name
I am a lamb, I am, I am
I belong to Jesus.

Jesus can only be the Good Shepherd if He has some sheep. "We are his people, and the sheep of his pasture" (Psalm 100:3). Good shepherds feed and lead their sheep. Taking care of us—that's what makes Jesus the Good Shepherd.

We did not force Jesus into this role as Shepherd of the sheep. We did not elect Him by popular vote. He volunteered. He laid down His life for the sheep.

We are in the middle of an enigma wrapped in a mystery, coronavirus and volatile stock markets and unemployment and schools dismissed.

Don't forget who you are in all of this. You have a Good Shepherd who watches over the food, the fences, and the future.

Scripture Reading: Psalm 100

Prayer: *Dear God, I face some big challenges today. I want my heart and mind to be in sync with Your will and purpose. Guide me as I make decisions. Feed my soul. Thank You for being my Good Shepherd.*

Day 5

A friend gave me two big bags of bass fillets this week. The gift reminded me of a fishing trip where I learned an important lesson.

I was combat fishing in the Russian River in Alaska some years ago. Combat fishing happens when everyone fishes in the same spot. The red salmon were running, and the silver salmon had begun to come up the river.

I made my way into the middle of the pack of fishermen. I was fishing at the very point where the clear waters of the Russian River met the gray waters of the Kenai River.

I saw a flash of pink as a big fish churned in the water, and then I saw my line heading downstream. That line was twenty-five-pound test line. The line was not going to break. But my spool was not locking. I pushed my thumb down to stop the whining spool and burned a blister on my thumb. I tried to reel, but the fish was too strong. He just kept stripping line off the spool.

Fishermen began to jump back and curse as my line got tangled with theirs. I slogged through the stream, water running over my wading boots, and tried again, unsuccessfully, to hold the fish. He was fifty yards downstream, and every fisherman between me and that fish was beginning to tangle up in my line.

I tried to reel him in once more, but he was still running. Only five or ten feet of line was left on the whole spool. If he ripped it to the end I would be out of fishing for the day, my new fishing line all gone. With my pole bent double, I cried out down the bank, "Someone cut the line." And someone did.

Have you ever caught a fish that was bigger than your tackle? Have you ever tackled a job and, halfway through, realized that you did not have the necessary tools to finish?

Occasionally we experience this sensation in our work as Christians. We feel ill-equipped, inadequate, and unable to do the job that we know needs done. We need to check our tackle box. We have better tackle than we realize.

Scripture: 2 Timothy 1:3–12

Prayer: *Show me, Lord, all the resources You have placed at my disposal to accomplish your work. Help my church to be fully equipped for the challenge of these strange days. May our members respond to Your call with faith and confidence in You.*

Day 6

I woke up at 1:30 the next morning thinking about that fish. When I said, "Cut the line," I thought it was the gracious and sensible thing to do. In retrospect, however, I wish I had thrown down that useless rod, grabbed the line with my bare hands, and hauled that monster in. It would have been a scene like that in Ernest Hemingway's *The Old Man and the Sea*. I should have stayed with that salmon as he towed me down the shoreline. I should have wrapped that line around my body and pulled hand over hand. Finally, with bloody hands and a tangled mass of line, I might have landed that feisty fish. Probably not. But maybe. At least I wouldn't have had to worry about the wisdom of cutting the line.

I lay in the bed for a long while, unable to sleep. And I asked the Lord, "Why can't I get this silly fish out of my head?" *Maybe I am supposed to learn something from that fish,* I thought, so I asked myself: "Are you the kind of man who cuts the line when things get tough?"

The big ones usually get away, not because they outfox us, but because they outlast us. The big ones get away, not because we lack the skill to win, but because we lack the will to win. The big ones often get away, not because we are too weak, but because we quit too soon.

It is always easier to cut the line. You are not absolutely certain that you can land that fish anyway. You have folks around you upset because your big project has interrupted their plans. They don't think you can get the job done, and you are doubtful. Too often when the going gets tough, we cut the line.

Tough times like these give birth to some of the most powerful and creative ideas and projects. Necessity really is the mother of invention. God is using this seedbed of social distancing and economic turbulence to bring forth something new in me and you, and in our churches and communities.

Are you about to cut the line on something you really believe is of God? If so, I urge you to hold on and see God do His best work in you.

Scripture: 1 Corinthians 2:6–12

Prayer: *Give me endurance, Lord, for the great tasks You give me. And give me wisdom to know when to hang on, regardless of the pain, and when to cut the line.*

Day 7

Rebekah, my middle child ("Middlest," I call her), was a young teenager when she charged into the kitchen one morning. She had decided that she was hungry. I heard some knocking around in the kitchen, the pulling of drawers and rustling of pans. She was not well acquainted with the kitchen, actually.

Finally she called out, "How long does it take to boil an egg?" I heard her, and I laughed to myself.

Her mother replied from a [safe] distance, "About three minutes."

"I haven't got that kind of time," she replied curtly, and proceeded to a "faster" food—probably a peanut butter sandwich or cold cereal.

No time for a three-minute egg? I thought with amazement. *Is this the same teenager who can sleep until 1 p.m. and crawl out of bed yawning?*

Not only teenagers, but many adults, feel the press of time and the hurry of the pace. During this pandemic we are experiencing, many people are marking time anxiously, losing precious moments with family members while they pace back and forth, waiting for things to "get back to normal." What is it that we are rushing through life to get to? I am not sure we know.

Preparations for the Passover meal in the Old Covenant took two weeks and involved every person in the house. The meal was prepared as a group experience. They savored the time together in the kitchen. These were busy people, just like us, but their celebration of God's deliverance required a lengthy reprieve—something like what we are getting in our "stay-at-home" season.

The people of God in the Old Covenant were willing to take time for a "three-minute egg," and we are wise to do the same. We rush by the sweetest moments of our lives, captured by uncertain futures that seem to us more important than the present. Something about this careening toward the future does not make sense, and we know it in our saner moments.

Scripture: Psalm 118

Prayer: *Creator God, keep me tuned in to the present even as I remember the past and envision the future. Help me to celebrate the gift of life this day and savor with gratitude the moments with loved ones that are part of this season.*

Day 8

I taught the Bible and led worship in a Texas prison every week for six years. Most of the time I was on death row.

Early in my prison ministry, I participated in a weekend event. I was assigned to a cell block with about fifty male prisoners. It was my first time to be the only volunteer on a cell block.

The guard left me standing in the exercise room where muscle-bound men pumped heavy weights. The door clanged shut behind me, and I was suddenly afraid. I did not know these people. Why was I risking bodily harm to talk to them? What was I thinking?

The guard was gone. There was no turning back. I spoke to a couple men lifting weights, but they ignored me. I walked toward the back, looking for someone to talk to. I reached the sleeping quarters with bunk beds in tight rows.

As my face appeared in the doorway of the bunkhouse, a voice called out in the semi-darkness, "Pastor Crosby!"

I turned and saw a young man sitting on a top bunk. His name was Steve. He attended a church in Gladewater, Texas, where I served as pastor for four years. He was probably twelve years old when I left that church. I had not seen him or heard anything about him for many years.

But I was happy to see him! Suddenly I felt as though I was in the company of friends, not strangers, and my fear disappeared. I stayed more than an hour in that cell block. Several men prayed to receive Christ as I shared with them the wonderful gospel of Jesus and His love.

A great truth gripped me in the midst of it all, and I have reflected upon it many times since. Those inmates were not strange people from another planet. They were our sons and daughters, brothers and sisters.

We must not forget the thousands of men and women in prison, especially those in the prisons near us. Part of the indication that you are truly God's child is this: "I was in prison and you came to me" (Matthew 25:36). They are included in Jesus' parable of the forgotten and outcast who are cared for by His true followers: the hungry, the thirsty, the stranger, the naked, the sick, and the prisoner. We are called by our Lord to treat them as people of great worth in His sight.

The United States incarcerates more people per capita than any other jurisdiction in the world. The vast majority of these prisoners live in tight quarters where the coronavirus could easily spread. If you are anxious about contracting this disease, think how anxious the prisoners might be.

Scripture: Psalm 8

Prayer: *Remind me, Lord, of the dignity of every human life. Help me to treat others—old and young, rich and poor—with respect because they are Your creations and the objects of Your love. Forgive me when I seek to elevate myself by putting down others. Be with the prisoners today. Calm their fears. Increase their faith. Bless the staff and volunteers who attend to them.*

Day 9

Rebekah and her two sons, Brady and Graham, ages nine and seven, drove from New Orleans to stay awhile.

We went fishing in Aunt Dianne's oldest stock tanks, the ones that never go dry. Aunt Dianne didn't know whether there were any fish in them or not, but they were a better alternative than Uncle Charles's tanks that dry up in droughts.

We dug worms in the garden, finding two dozen, mostly long and thin. We loaded the 2002 Explorer, Uncle Josh's old vehicle, with two tackle boxes bought at garage sales and two-and-a-half poles (Graham's is only three feet long). We took a stringer and a casting net, being optimistic.

We hooked up the sixteen-foot trailer, despite one taillight not working because I hit forward instead of sideways on the zero-turn lawnmower. We found the ramps, knocked off the fire ants, and loaded the ATV in case we needed to joyride, which we did.

We hadn't gone two steps at the first tank before we disturbed a foot-long snake. The presence of snakes became a dominant theme, along with spiders and wasps.

The fishing was great once we decided that Papa (that's me) would do all the casting. Before that we spent our time unwrapping fishing line from mesquite trees. Graham caught himself two bass big enough to keep. We caught eight perch or sunfish or bluegill—those hand-sized, multi-colored fish—really beautiful—that manage to inhabit practically every body of water. I saw some iteration of the species in a pool of water captured by huge branches fifty feet off the ground in a rain forest in Costa Rica.

I love Graham's optimism. His cork was sitting there doing nothing. I said, "Graham, bring it in and see if you still have some worm on the hook."

He started to wind in his line, muttering, "I'm going to see if there's a fish on my hook." Well, there could have been.

A pandemic helped make this memory. Look for the silver lining. His mercies are new every morning (Lamentations 3:23).

Scripture: John 21:1–12 (a fishing trip)

Prayer: *God of all mercies, help me look for fish today, not worms. Show me Your handiwork amid the quarantine turbulence. Give me a grateful heart. You are good all the time.*

Day 10

I am trying to think of the number two trillion. I wonder if anyone on Capitol Hill can actually fathom that number of dollars. Where do you go to get that kind of money?

One hundred billion stars shine in our Milky Way galaxy. That's a lot of stars, but it's nowhere close to two trillion.

Here it is: the observable universe is estimated to contain 200 billion to *two trillion galaxies.*

Go with the larger estimate, two trillion galaxies. And I thought the dollars were piling up. For every dollar in the largest stimulus package in human history, God made a galaxy with 100 billion stars, or so.

It's too early in the morning. I can't get my mind around it. Not to worry. God knows the name of every star.

And God knows the name of every person on earth. He knows their physical and emotional condition. He knows how vulnerable they are to the coronavirus.

God knows how many hospital beds and ventilators are needed. He knows the number of N-95 masks it takes to protect our medical professionals. He knows the worldwide need for PPE (personal protection equipment).

God knows, and God cares.

Two trillion galaxies do not distract the Almighty from giving you full attention when you pray. You are always welcome in the control room of this universe, and God knows your name before you whisper His.

This is the wonder of prayer, connecting to the center of all existence everywhere and finding there the One who created all things, including you, whose fundamental essence is love.

We humans must do all we can to protect the image-bearers of God on this planet. Every human is of infinite worth.

We do not have to do this work alone, however. We join with the Creator God every moment we serve others.

Go ahead. Speak His name. There may be two trillion galaxies, but "he is not far from any one of us" (Acts 17:27 NIV).

> From one man he made all the nations, that they should inhabit the whole earth; and he marked out their appointed times in history and the boundaries of their lands. God did this so that they would seek him and perhaps reach out for him and find him, though he is not far from any one of us. "For in him we live and move and have our being." As some of your own poets have said, "We are his offspring." —Acts 17:26–28

Scripture Reading: Acts 17:16–31

Prayer: *Almighty God, thank You for attending to our needs. I am so glad You love us! Help us, Heavenly Father. We need You desperately right now all over this earth. Give us the wisdom we need to fight this pandemic. Protect those on the front lines of this battle. Give us great hope and faith. Increase our love for one another.*

Day 11

I picked up two old tractor tires yesterday from the place where I bought new ones a couple months ago. Old tires are expensive to get rid of, so they send them home with the owner of the new tires. I pass the business establishment several times a week and finally remembered to pick them up while I was towing a trailer.

The tires were sitting outside and were full of rainwater. We'd had about four inches over several days. I laid them flat, and water poured out. I picked them up, bounced them, and more water sloshed out.

The last little bit of water is hard to get out of a tire. It just keeps sloshing around and around instead of jumping out. I threw the first tire into the trailer when it still had that stubborn water residue. The tire hit perfectly flat and threw that icky water right in my face.

My grandsons had a belly laugh, looking at me in my astonishment, dripping wet. My only comfort—I was already sticky and stinky from digging worms and handling fish.

The world is an interesting place. Something new happens every day that reminds you how little you know. Two trillion galaxies out there full of surprises, and I can't empty the water from an old tire without getting soaked.

Sometimes I feel like a bug floating in that water, sloshing around, everything beyond my control and capacity. That's when I have to remind myself that my significance in this universe is not derived from my capacity, intelligence, wealth, or appearance. Even when I am dirty and dripping, doused by my own mistakes, "Jesus loves me, this I know, for the Bible tells me so."

You never get too old for that message.

Scripture: Philippians 2:1–11

Prayer: *Father in heaven, thank You for caring for me despite my foibles. Let your love so pour through me that I may be freed of my self-occupation and truly interested in others. Bless my efforts and others' efforts as we seek to be faithful to our churches and communities while maintaining social distancing. Be with those who are sick and the medical professionals who minister to their needs.*

Day 12

It is said Saddam Hussein had all of his food checked for poison during the Gulf War. I do not doubt he feared such intrigue. The food we eat both strengthens us and makes us vulnerable to poisoning.

King Pharaoh of Egypt had a "cupbearer," a servant personally responsible for his refreshing beverage. The king of Babylon had a similar position in his close circle of confidants. One of the things the cupbearer did occasionally was check for poison by tasting food or drink before it reached the king.

A friend asked me this week to evaluate a theological statement and give my opinion of its nature: poisonous or innocuous. Pastors are cupbearers. We pass the cup during the communion observance. Pastors are expected to provide spiritual sustenance and guidance for their churches.

The local pastor often tests the menu for members. "Taste this," the person will say, "and tell me if it's poisonous." The pastor is expected to be able to "smell out" the poison in the idea, teaching, or thought. I fulfill my role as a cupbearer when I test a certain spiritual food and give my opinion of its nutritional value or poisonous content.

My pastoral taste buds started screaming when I heard the comments of Texas Lieutenant Governor Dan Patrick that grandparents would be willing to die for the US economy. Even in macroeconomics we cannot put a price on a human life.

The sacrifice of children and the elderly is often seen as an economic solution, but not by God's people. Jesus taught the full dignity and infinite worth of every human life. Keeping a preborn child may be expensive. But it is the right thing to do.

The same goes for the elderly.

The minute we put a price tag on a human life we have devalued that person and elevated ourselves above them. We have dehumanized them, made them less human than ourselves. We have turned them into a commodity, a thing to be bartered to buy ourselves what we think is a better life.

Good intentions cannot rescue a bad idea. Sacrificing the very young or the very old to improve our economy is forbidden by the God who made us and loves us all.

Scripture: Psalm 139:13–18

Prayer: *Thank You, Heavenly Father, for Your infinite grace and wisdom. Help me to treat others as the image-bearers of God, especially those who are vulnerable. Help me carry Your Word as I go about my day. Give me an expectant heart so that I will not miss any opportunity to bring You glory through my life.*

Day 13

Graham discovered the rain peppering down at our house one morning. He was looking for it, since rain was in the forecast, and he had just asked me where the rain was.

The forecast of rain is the reason I made a solo trip the previous night back to the stock tank where we'd fished at sunset. In Central Texas we build "tanks"—ponds dug in the earth that provide water to our "stock"—cows, sheep, horses, and goats. It's a regional colloquialism.

This tank was built on a draw in the hill decades ago. Mesquite trees on the berm, old and twisted, bobbed in the beam of the flashlight. They snagged my clothes as I wove my way in the dark toward our fishing spot.

I found my cell phone lying in the grass near the water. Brady had used it to take a picture of Graham and his catch, and neither of us had remembered to pick it up when we left.

I stopped for a moment, startled by the warbling croak of a frog in the cattails. The wind had laid. The water did not stir. I turned off the flashlight. I could hear no cars and see no lights. The frog was joined by others—a chorus of frogs singing in the night. Nature had completely invaded this manmade pond.

The moment felt familiar. My father took me fishing at night on the lakes of Minnesota when I was only seven or eight years old. The world is mysterious at night and can be scary, especially if you are alone. Sounds seem amplified, and familiar objects become ominous shapes. But if your father is there by your side, you know you are okay.

Today is strange for us. Our routines have been interrupted now for weeks. Reports of a spreading virus come from everywhere.

"How are you doing?" we ask in a phone call.

"We're okay. I had a cough and was tested for the virus. We've had two confirmed cases here in Abilene." We are concerned that we may contract a disease that can be fatal. Our prayers are filled with petitions for protection and healing for those we love and those on the front lines of this battle.

A pall has fallen over the land, a darkness of uncertainty and fear. It affects individuals, families, communities and nearly all human institutions.

The God of all comfort is with us in this journey. If your Heavenly Father is there by your side, you know you are okay.

Scripture: Philippians 4:4–9

Prayer: *Thank You, Father, for making this journey with us. Thank You for the peace you give us in difficult times. Help me to walk with You today, practicing Your presence with every word and deed.*

Day 14

I learned a valuable lesson yesterday when the boys—my grandsons—and I went fishing. The fifth stock tank on Aunt Dianne's place is called the Garden Tank. I had never seen it.

We saw Uncle Charles at Head's Hardware where we took the trailer to replace a blown tire. We use the trailer to transport the ATV. Riding the ATV in the pasture is almost as much fun as catching fish.

Uncle Charles told us that there was a boat at the Garden Tank.

"A boat! Oh, Papa, let's go," the boys said loud enough for all the old men in the store to hear.

So we did, because of the boat. I did not know that they had never really been in a boat, being city boys.

The Garden Tank is amazing. Many years ago they dammed up what we would call a mountain gorge. The berm is probably twenty-five feet high, and the gorge is beautiful. Slabs of rock make a great place to fish from the shore. Trees line the shore. The tank is at least three or four acres of surface. It's deep and clear and just the very best tank we'd ever seen.

I turned over the flat-bottom aluminum boat lying on the shore, checking for snakes. The boys helped. We got a couple of branches to push and row, loaded up, and scooted out into the water.

All of a sudden, the boys were terrified. They started to scream, "It's too deep. It's going to turn over! We're going too far! We're gonna drown! Papa, take us back!"

I rowed back to shore, puzzled by their outbursts. They were truly afraid.

We are experiencing something new in our country and our communities. We have never had this kind of event in my lifetime. Part of the anxiety and fear is because this is something new that we have never done before.

God said through his prophet (Isaiah 43:2): "When you pass through the waters, I will be with you; and through the rivers, they shall not overwhelm you."

Scripture: Isaiah 40:1–5

Prayer: *Dear Lord, I am trying to navigate these waters. I need Your help. Please increase my faith. Help me to be steady in these times. Give me wisdom in my conversation and decisions. Help me to know what I need to do and what I need to release. I'm trusting You!*

Day 15

I woke up this morning worried about *Setophaga chrysoparia*. I have to worry about something. It's my nature.

The golden-cheeked warbler, its common name, breeds only in Central Texas along the edge of the Edwards Plateau. Its population is declining, so it's listed as endangered. An adult male weighs a third of an ounce.

I own property in the breeding area of this small creature. A large construction project is planned, which would be a good thing financially.

A crew walked the property last Friday looking for this bird. I don't know if they found one or not. These birds migrate to Mexico in the winter. Maybe they are staying longer than usual—social distancing.

God knows and cares about this warbler. "Are not two sparrows sold for a penny?" Jesus asked. "And not one of them will fall to the ground apart from your Father. But even the hairs of your head are all numbered. Fear not, therefore; you are of more value than many sparrows" (Matthew 10:29–31).

Jesus comforts me by affirming that my worth is much greater than a bird. Yet He also affirms the value of the bird. How does a nesting warbler compare to a human project?

We weigh these values in our minds all the time as we make decisions and try to do what is right and best and good. Jesus might want us to stop the project to protect the bird. But there is no doubt about this—He laid down His life for sinners like us.

Scripture: Matthew 10:26–39

Prayer: *Hello, Father. I am talking to You today while facing more days of quarantine. Help me maintain my sanity and Your priorities for me. Give me wisdom as I try to provide for my family while keeping everybody safe. Be with those who have lost their jobs. And be with those who are sick.*

Day 16

Digging worms is fun. We really get into it. Everyone has a tool—shovel or rake or hoe. The grandsons swing their tools vigorously. I have to calm them down, tell them to be careful, or they will clobber me.

Digging worms is fun even though, or maybe because, the worms thrive in the shower drain.

We live in a country home on several acres. The man who renovated the house decided to let all the gray water drain into the yard instead of into the septic tank.

Worms must love Head and Shoulders shampoo. And the boys love breaking up the clods, rummaging through the soil, and pulling out those wiggly worms grown large in the moist earth.

Riding the four-wheeler is fun. Making trips into the pasture in the ATV to check on the sheep is fun. Of course, fishing is fun.

School online is not fun.

Their mother announces that it is time for school, and those boys are transformed from high-energy worm-diggers, laughing and squealing, into sad little fellows suffering persecution, unjustly treated, forced into hard labor.

Discipline is a big part of "disciple." As disciples of Jesus Christ, we are called to lay aside other pursuits and follow Him as the center of our lives. The Christian life includes the disciplines of prayer and Bible study.

Our goal in reading and learning God's Word is not to become scholars but to become faithful disciples. When we practice these basic disciplines we mature in Christ, becoming more like our Master and Teacher in our words and deeds.

We are all developing alternative schedules in these days of quarantine. We know that part of each day should be spent in prayer and in the Word of God.

Let's be faithful disciples in this season. Let's find a rhythm that brings us to the throne room. And let's expect that prayer and Bible reading will be even more delightful than digging worms.

Scripture: 2 Timothy 3:1–17

Prayer: *Help me be a faithful student of Your Word, delighted in my personal devotions and excited by my Bible study. Help me learn Your Word so that I may teach others. Make me powerful in prayer for those I know are lost.*

Day 17

I heard the chickens flapping yesterday and saw them running before I spied the chicken hawk soaring low over the flock. It has been more than a year since just such a hawk dropped down among the chicks, snatched one up, and carried it off in his talons.

The chickens will run for shelter whenever a big bird passes overhead. If I want to drive them back to the barn, I take off my hat and wave it like an attacking hawk. It scares them worse than anything.

Living creatures are designed with an instinct for survival. A worm will resist the point of a hook. A tiny fish will flip its way back to the water.

Your friends and neighbors may wear masks when they go to the grocery store. I made a quick trip yesterday and noticed three masks in the small Dollar store. We did not see one at Disney World months ago when we visited while the virus was still mostly overseas.

The protocols are changing. People are keeping their distance, washing their hands, and sanitizing surfaces. It is the instinct for self-preservation at work in the people around us and in ourselves.

We do good when we prevent sickness and suffering and minister to those who are afflicted. In all of our medical practice we work to "do no harm" and to give the gift of health and life.

The psalmist said, "I shall not die, but I shall live, and recount the deeds of the LORD" (Psalm 118:17). He was under attack from his enemies. They surrounded him, and he thought he would be overcome. But God intervened on his behalf. He wrote: "The Lord is God, and he has made his light to shine upon us. Bind the festal sacrifice with cords, up to the horns of the altar!" (Psalm 118:27).

You can see in these words the entry of Jesus into Jerusalem on Palm Sunday when He was hailed as the Messiah. The Messiah means light and salvation. He shines his light around us. He brings life, not death.

We are fighting this coronavirus with the light God has given us. The understanding of sickness and disease is dramatically increased in our day. We have drugs and procedures to help us in sickness that previous generations never imagined.

We celebrate these medical advances by giving God praise for creative thinking, scientific knowledge, capable hands, and the gift of life.

We embrace Jesus as Messiah because He brings to us life—abundant and eternal.

Scripture: Psalm 118:13–23

Prayer: *Dear God, help our scientists and physicians as they combat this disease. Help us find the vaccine we need. Be with those who have fallen ill. Give us wisdom as we test medicines. We give You praise in all circumstances, and we promise to praise You for every healing touch that comes our way.*

Day 18

Ellis Marsalis has succumbed to the coronavirus. He was a wonderful man and terrific musician, patriarch of the Marsalis family in New Orleans.

He was our featured jazz musician for three successive Christmas programs at First Baptist New Orleans. He brought his team, including his nephew, who played the xylophone. Ellis played the piano marvelously with great feeling and slow rhythm.

Ellis partnered with Harry Connick Jr. to sponsor Musician's Village in the Upper Ninth Ward of New Orleans after Hurricane Katrina devastated the area in 2005. Our church had launched that project before the storm as the Baptist Crossroads Project. Ellis and Harry made it a media event that attracted such donors as President George W. Bush and Miami Heat star Dwyane Wade (who gave me a pair of his *signature* basketball shoes, which nobody in the gym believed). Habitat for Humanity became the largest homebuilder in New Orleans post-Katrina, and Baptist Crossroads was their partner on 91 houses.

Pastor Peter quoted Isaiah 40:6–8 in his letter to followers of Jesus (1 Peter 1:24–25 NIV): "'All people are like grass, and all their glory is like the flowers of the field; the grass withers and the flowers fall, but the word of the Lord endures forever.' And this is the word that was preached to you."

No matter who a person is or what they accomplish, eventually they pass from this life. Jacob told his children: "I am about to be gathered to my people. Bury me with my fathers in the cave in the field of Ephron the Hittite" (Genesis 49:29 NIV).

We speak of death, not because we are morbid or negative in our thinking, but because it is a reality of life that all people must face, including people of faith.

Peter preached a message from God's Word. His first sermon after the first Easter was recorded by Doctor Luke in Acts 2. Peter told thousands of people, "God has raised this Jesus to life, and we are all witnesses of it" (Acts 2:32 NIV).

This is the Word of God—Jesus raised from the dead—that gives eternal hope to all who believe.

Scripture: 1 Peter 1

Prayer: *Father in Heaven, focus my mind and heart upon Your Word today. Help me see my world and my community through Your eyes. Be with all who are mourning today. Help them turn their hearts toward You.*

Day 19

I went with out my grandsons, Brady and Graham, after dark last night to take care of the chickens and sheep. We had gotten absorbed in a television show and forgot to do it before sunset.

Brady and I wore tennis shoes. Graham found his boots. We climbed into the ATV and drove up the hill and across the yard to the barn. We hopped out, went inside, fed the sheep, and closed the chicken coop.

Graham's flashlight was nearly out, and Brady was using the spotlight to survey the pasture. The boys were already back in the ATV when I decided to check for eggs. *The white hen is setting,* I think. She was still on the nest.

I reached out to close the big door when the light bobbed in front of me, and I saw a circular shape on the ground. It gave me pause, and I shouted for a light.

A rattlesnake was curled up a foot or two outside the barn door, right where we were walking. His rattle was moving slightly but made no noise. His head was in the alert position in the center of his coils, low and looking at me. I keep a shovel in the barn for just this reason. I plunged it and delivered a fatal blow.

I knew there had to be rattlesnakes on this Central Texas mountain, but that is the first one I've seen on our home property. We are now on red alert around here, all sobered up. We watch our steps and wear our boots when we go outside.

Protective gear like boots are truly essential when rattlers are a possibility. I've got three pair, counting the ones that got wet that I am trying to deodorize.

I appreciate more fully now the dilemma of our doctors and nurses. Our medical professionals must wear personal protective equipment (PPE) in this coronavirus pandemic.

Antivenom is 99 percent effective against a snakebite, but we have no cure for the virus.

Scripture: Psalm 18:1–3

Prayer: *Dear God, be with our medical professionals today as they deliver care in such a difficult season. Protect them from harm. Help us with the shortage of medical equipment here and around the world. Give wisdom and success to those who are working on this problem. We place ourselves in Your hands.*

Day 20

We recently baked a birthday cake for nobody. We sang the birthday song to nobody, and we ate more cake than we should have. My wife, Janet, makes the best carrot cake in our galaxy.

The decision to bake the cake was just about firm when Graham noticed our problem.

"We are baking a birthday cake for nobody," he observed. Up to that moment we had not realized that this was a birthday cake. We began to think about our loved ones.

"April had a birthday," Rebekah said, but it was over.

"Rachel has a birthday this month," Nina said, but it was weeks away. We thought about calling her to let her know that we were baking a cake for her birthday, but we didn't follow through.

We baked the birthday cake for nobody, who is a really good person, we decided as we devoured the cake. Everybody knew nobody, it turned out, and could recount his good qualities.

It was an exercise in imagination without borders, really fun and funny. We laughed and ate and sang the song to nobody at least three times. We created the narrative together, building on the contributions of others as thoughts turned into words.

The birthday cake for nobody will probably become part of family lore, counterbalancing the memory of the rattlesnake that scared us to death shortly after the party.

"A merry heart doeth good like a medicine," goes Proverbs 17:22 in the KJV, "but a broken spirit drieth the bones."

Both the amusing and the menacing are aspects of daily life. We cannot help but be anxious about the coronavirus, and its presence casts a shadow over our hearts and our world.

We cannot relinquish the laughter and fun, for that is the best medicine in a world like ours.

We need some play therapy today. Brighten up your smile. Wake up that merry heart. Sing a song, tell a story, and see how the medicine works.

Scripture: Proverbs 17:22–28

Prayer: *Lord Jesus, I want Your joy. Help me to have a merry heart as I go about my day. Help me see Your presence in my life, and give me Your peace.*

Day 21

I stood at the crest of the Mount of Olives for the first time, drinking it all in. People in my group chatted and took pictures, but I surveyed the scene before me. The Dome of the Rock is the most prominent building in Jerusalem. It is built on the Temple Mount at the center of the city.

The slope of the Mount of Olives is fairly steep. The mountain plunges hundreds of feet downward into a gorge, the Kidron Valley. The Temple Mount rises on the other side.

I imagined Jesus riding a donkey with throngs of people who sang and waved palm branches. I imagined His disciples walking near Him as He rode, amazed by the crowd and their enthusiasm for Jesus.

The skeptics were there too, in my mind, as I looked at the mountain. They walked along with Jesus and the disciples, astonished that the crowd would hail Jesus as King. They urged Jesus to rebuke the crowd and stop the blasphemy.

Jesus told them all, "If they keep quiet, the stones will cry out" (Luke 19:40 NIV).

The mountain is littered with stones. Bedrock protrudes in layers down the entire slope of the mountain.

Today the mountain is also covered in tombs—thousands and thousands of tombs. And the tombs are marked with stones. Some of the tombs are small buildings, elaborate in their stonework. The hand-carved stones are just as prominent on the Mount of Olives as the scattered stones beside the roads.

Many craftsmen worked long hours to carve these stones over many generations. The Hebrews buried their dead here on this mount until a vast cemetery was formed dating back three thousand years. More than 150,000 Hebrew graves crowd the mountainside, from the tomb of Absalom, King David's son, not far from the Kidron Brook, to the tomb of former Israeli prime minister Menachem Begin.

The scattered stones would have filled the air with praise had the people refused to do so on that day of Jesus' Triumphal Entry into Jerusalem. But these monuments to the dead would have cried out as well. The memorial stones for the prophets Haggai, Zachariah, and Malachi are here, and they, along with thousands of others in these graves, anticipated the coming of the Messiah one day.

We join with all creation, including the stones, when we acknowledge that Jesus is the long-awaited Messiah, King of kings, and Savior of the world.

Scripture: Luke 19:28–40

Prayer: *Messiah Jesus, I join with the crowd who hailed You. I praise You and proclaim You as King of all kings and Lord of my life.*

Day 22

As we admired the flight of the waterfowl, my son Joshua was distracted by motion in the tall grass. A young armadillo made his way noisily along the shore, scratching and rooting for bugs. He was too deaf and blind to notice us at first, but then he suddenly rocked back on his hind legs, lifted his long nose in the air, and tried to identify a new smell.

I moved slowly toward the armadillo, scheming to grab him by the tail. "What are you doing?" asked Joshua. I realized then that he had never captured a live armadillo. His education was sorely deficient. "Will it bite you?" he asked warily.

"No. It may scratch me if I let it," I replied, and broke into a gallop as the creature took off toward the water. I lunged and fell full length in the dirt, a bull nettle in my hand instead of the armored tail.

The armadillo made a turn into a hollowed tree trunk at the water's edge. It began to dig futilely at a shallow hole under the tree, mistakenly fearful for its life.

The morning breaks with a breathtaking splash of red and orange, the waterfowl rise in a blur of graceful energy, the vapors of divine breath wrap every plant and tree. And where is man? Often studying a damp, dark corner with his back to the dawn, looking for an escape from some imaginary foe. The little animal clawing the rotten wood is a metaphor of our times.

Make no mistake. God said creation was "very good," and He rested contentedly. The sin of man has not erased the beauty of creation. The damage sin has done is mostly internal, causing us to scurry to the rotting hole and miss the dazzling light.

If you perceive life to be ugly or boring, what needs adjusted is not "out there" but in you. After Jesus Christ does his heart work, the handiwork of God comes alive every day.

Scripture: Psalm 136:1–9

Prayer: *Thank You, Creator God, for the beauty of the earth, and thank You for the beauty of Your holiness. Help me to think less about the darkness and more about the light. Help me today to rejoice in my salvation even as I seek to address the trouble of my time.*

Day 23

"**D**id you know Jesus is coming back?" Wes asked his grandmother. In his seven years he could not remember a time when he had more important news to deliver to a more important person. He asked the question with an undisguised air of importance, and his grandmother could imagine him standing tall as he held the telephone and asked this question. She wanted to hug him, but he was in Virginia, and he wanted an answer, not a hug.

Mae paused for a moment, then gave her reply.

"Yes, Weston, I knew that."

With a note of impatience and a trace of irritation, the little boy responded, "Now just how long have you known that?" Wes proceeded then to describe for his grandmother some of the details concerning the soon-coming event of which he had just been informed. The awesome nature of this earth-shaking news had captured his imagination.

Wes was checking the sky regularly for days, I am sure, looking up from the playground or swimming pool to see if a glorious glow was leaping from cloud to cloud, expecting Jesus to descend momentarily from His throne in heaven.

This expectation of the Second Coming is akin to the Jewish expectation in Jesus' day of the coming of Messiah. Devout Jews, trapped under the heel of Rome, longed for the day when the King would come. This expectation was the reason a throng gathered on the Mount of Olives to proclaim Jesus as king.

Hard times remind us that this world is not our permanent home, that Jesus is coming again to receive us into His presence.

A little child must lead us again. Jesus is putting His arm around Wes's shoulders as He turns to us and says, "Whoever does not receive the kingdom of God like a child shall not enter it" (Mark 10:15). Wes stands on tiptoe beside Peter and John as they examine the heavens for the first glimpse of their returning King.

Scripture: Luke 21:5–36

Prayer: *Help me, Lord, to receive with childlike faith the promise of Your coming. Forgive me when I doubt the truth You so plainly teach. Give me patience to wait and eagerness of heart to see the fulfillment of Your promise.*

Day 24

The more dignified and astute took a bench near the observatory, opened a good novel, and allowed the kids to gawk at the comets and falling stars. Their startled outbursts arrested us no longer; we had heard such outbursts for years.

"He is coming," we acknowledged as the children jumped with excitement, "but it could be a thousand years. The stars have been falling for a long time."

God had gotten Wes's attention with an age-old truth that flew for him like a new kite. He was now on tiptoe, looking for the appearing of our Lord, and all that he had was God's promise.

How does God get us back on tiptoe when the truth starts to wear like an old garment, when it stays in the closet because it is outdated? He stirs the heart with personal encounters. He rides upon the wind and waves. The ground convulses at His bidding, and fire leaps from the heart of the earth. Some people in this earth give God their full attention.

Wes said, "How long have you known that?" Riveted by the simple truth of Christ's return, the seven-year-old spoke accusingly to all of us for whom this truth has grown old. How many others, old and young, would be glued to the spyglass if similar news were delivered to them? This truth that kept the apostles craning their necks will do the same for multitudes caught in falling ash and quaking earth and spinning hurricanes and rampaging plague.

Jesus is coming! This lurching world will not finally disintegrate without hope. Jesus is coming! The vomiting volcano, the devouring famine, the staggering violence, the frightened and fleeing masses, the coronavirus pandemic—He has left us here to be light in the ash cloud.

Tell them sooner. They will believe. Jesus is coming!

Scripture: 1 Thessalonians 4:13—5:11

Prayer: *Give me courage, Lord, in a skeptical age, to share the truth of Your soon return. Help me to embrace this truth myself. Show me how it should change my life today in some way. Give me an understanding of the future You plan for me and all humans so I may know how to handle the present.*

Day 25

Vanilla and Oreo were born March 18 and March 20, respectively, in our two-acre pasture. Oreo is a buck and is black with a white face and a white tip on his tail. Vanilla is a ewe lamb and is all white.

Vanilla and Oreo have fun all day, running and jumping and butting heads. We have watched them bounce so high, forward and backward, like they were on trampolines, and marveled that they could keep their footing.

The lambs discovered it was fun to chase chickens, and they have been terrorizing the hens ever since.

My grandsons Brady and Graham feed the sheep and always try to catch the lambs. They have held the lambs in their arms and carried them around. The lambs are growing fast. Catching them and carrying them may be about over for the boys.

I suppose that Hebrew children through the generations have treated the Passover lambs like pets. The lambs are supposed to be separated from the flock a couple of weeks before the feast. Having them penned beside the house would make it convenient for the children to care for them.

Even today, during Passover, lambs all over the world are slaughtered. Many of the shepherds here in Central Texas sell their lambs during the great Jewish feast. The urban centers like New York and Houston are the big markets.

Our two lambs are perfect, as far as we can tell—no visible defects. They are beautiful animals, playful and innocent. Vanilla is female, so I intend to keep her. Oreo is a buck and will be sold when he weighs around one hundred pounds.

I have been teaching the boys about cattle. They can identify Herefords, Black Angus, and Holsteins. They know that the first two are raised for meat and the third one for milk. It has not occurred to them that sheep are also raised for meat.

It has been more than three thousand years since that first Passover in Egypt. Every generation of Hebrew children since the Exodus have grieved the loss of their beautiful lambs.

The Apostle Paul urged followers of Jesus to live a life worthy of their calling. He wrote in 1 Corinthians 5:7–8: "Get rid of the old yeast, so that you may be a new unleavened batch—as you really are. For Christ, our Passover lamb, has been sacrificed. Therefore let us keep the Festival, not with the old bread leavened with malice and wickedness, but with the unleavened bread of sincerity and truth" (NIV).

Given that Jesus was sacrificed on our behalf, how can we continue in a lifestyle of rebellion against God? We are compelled by His great gift of love to conform our lives to His great life by living in sincerity and truth.

Scripture: Exodus 12:1–20 (Passover instituted)

Prayer: *Father in Heaven, thank You for sending Your one and only Son to die on the Cross for my sin. Help me live for You today, practicing sincerity and truth with every word and deed.*

Day 26

The boys went barefoot to the barn yesterday. They had been swimming in a wading pool in the ninety-degree heat. They hopped on the ATVs, not thinking of snakes, and tooled right up the hill.

"Where are your boots," I said, not a question, when Brady opened the big barn door. He walked right in, as did Graham. We looked for snakes but, finding none, went about our business.

Soon the boys were in the pen with the sheep, bare-footed, toes squishing. Brady poured the sheep pellets into the trough.

"They'll step on your feet if you let them," I said, watching the ewes jostle for position. He handed me the scoop and eyed the lambs.

"Can I catch one?" he said, not waiting for an answer.

"Sure. I'm closing the gate to the pasture." I walked across the chicken yard thinking there was no way Brady could catch a lamb by himself.

"I caught him!" Brady yelled. I turned around to find Brady with Oreo in his arms.

We were leaving the barn when I noticed Graham's feet again.

"Brady has got to wash your feet today, and they're gonna be filthy." We had talked about them reenacting the foot-washing for my Wednesday evening Bible study. I had not planned for them to walk barefoot in the sheep pen, but there you go.

The disciples didn't know that Jesus was going to wash their feet. They made only the usual efforts to avoid animal droppings in the street. This was a real problem in urban areas, including in 1894 when *The Times* predicted, "In 50 years, every street in London will be buried under nine feet of manure."

Donkeys, cattle, sheep, goats, and an occasional horse or camel all used those streets in Jerusalem. The boys from Galilee probably never saw so much manure in one place. They plodded through it everywhere they went, including to the Upper Room.

We like to think when Jesus cleaned our souls He just had a little touching up to do. Not true. Our souls were as filthy as those disciples' feet. In fact, the prophet Isaiah gave us the famous saying, "All of us have become like one who is unclean, and all our righteous acts are like filthy rags" (Isaiah 64:6 NIV).

The soul becomes caked with filth when we, in arrogance and ignorance, suppose that our goodness excuses us from the need for God's mercy and forgiveness. Jesus did some awfully dirty work when He cleaned us within through His death upon the Cross.

Scripture: Romans 3:10–23

Prayer: *Dear Lord Jesus, thank You for dying on the Cross so that my sin could be taken away. Help me to remember this today. In all of my dealings with difficult and imperfect people, show me the depth of my own sin and my own great need for grace.*

Day 27

Our world knows about crosses and crucifixion almost exclusively because of the story of the crucifixion of Jesus Christ. Jesus' death upon the Cross has introduced generations of people to this Roman method of capital punishment. This approach to killing criminals was abandoned a long time ago, replaced by more efficient forms of execution, but the death of Jesus keeps the Cross in the center of our language.

A few years after Jesus' execution, the Cross became the symbol of Christianity. It appeared in art and literature and architecture. Thinking about the death of Christ and what it meant became the center of Christian theology.

Jesus introduced the Cross to His disciples some time before Good Friday—the day of the crucifixion of Jesus— and He did so in a most remarkable way. He introduced it as a symbol of being His disciple. He said, "Whoever does not take up his cross and follow me is not worthy of me" (Matthew 10:38).

Jesus spoke these words *before* He was executed on the Cross. He knew what was going to happen, but His disciples did not. He was preparing them for His death, but not in the usual way people prepare for the death of a loved one. Jesus was preparing them to understand His death as obedience to God. He followed God's path for Him as He went to the Cross, and they would follow God's path also when they took up their crosses every day. The cross of the disciple is his or her public identification with Jesus.

Scripture: Matthew 10:26–39

Prayer: *Dear Lord, I am amazed at the love You show for me on the Cross. Thank You for dying in my place. Thank You for laying down Your own life freely and willingly for me. Now help me, as Your disciple, to take up my cross and live my life fully committed to you.*

Day 28

We examined the cliff across the Colorado River for some time. We noticed a length of rope hanging across a rocky promontory. It had been abandoned there by climbers who had challenged the cliff some years earlier.

The bluff was about two hundred feet high. Two layers of rock were divided by a steep strip with grass and scrub trees. The rock layers were thirty to forty feet high and were occasionally broken by crevasses.

Our hosts told us that none of them had climbed the bluff before, so Joshua, Craig, and I decided to try.

We rowed across the river, landed our boat, and, with surprising success, climbed to the very top of that cliff. We scooted out to the edge of the protruding rock on top and enjoyed a new perspective on the country around us.

We could see the full bend of the Colorado River. We were higher than the road. We were at the top of that river valley.

Resurrection Day is the highest perspective we get in this life. From here, you can see where life comes from and where it goes. The cacti that dominate the landscape when you are climbing—I had a few imbedded needles—are scarcely visible here. The scrapes and strains that accompany any climb are quickly forgotten.

Easter is our highest peak spiritually. We soak in the view. We marvel at God's grace and power. We experience the exhilaration of God's mighty act on our behalf. We are full of hope and vision and anticipation.

Silent Saturday is also part of this special week. But Saturday has never been the same since Resurrection Sunday. Before Jesus, death was victor. Never had the grave been defeated. Somber Saturday seemed like the final comment on life. Then Jesus came out of the grave, and everything changed.

Scripture: 1 Corinthians 15:1–11

Prayer: *Hallelujah for the Cross and the empty tomb! Thank You, Jesus, for laying down Your life so we could really live. Thank You for the victory that is ours through Your resurrection!*

Day 29

Darkness can be a curse. One of the plagues on the land of Egypt that God sent to help free His people was three days of darkness.

Have you been in Carlsbad Caverns when they turn out the lights? The darkness is complete. You cannot see your hand in front of your face. Your eyes never adjust to the darkness. You are in complete darkness eight hundred feet below the surface of the earth. Spelunkers who lose their light often lose their lives. I saw rocks that were blackened by the lamps of the first explorers of Carlsbad. I saw their ladders still hanging high above me. And I imagined myself as a member of that spelunking team, having made my way miles from the mouth of the cave, exploring it for the first time. I imagined my lamp suddenly falling as I crept down a rocky cliff. I imagined that lamp crashing at the foot of the cliff and pitch darkness surrounding me. Like a blind man hanging on that cliff, my only hope would be another light.

Some people live in the darkness every day. They truly have no Heavenly Father. Like Paul described the Ephesians as "having no hope and without God in the world" (Ephesians 2:12), they have no transcendent purpose or meaning for their lives.

People lose their purpose for living. Strong, tough men come trembling, holding the divorce decree in their hands. They have lost their way. Others are devastated by the loss of a loved one and seem unable to find a reason for living in the wake of their loss.

Easter is the celebration of life and light. It is the announcement of our rescue. The truth of Easter dispels darkness in the mind and the shadow on the heart. The resurrection of Christ means that a loving God has acted on our behalf, that the Creator is also our Savior. We need no longer fear death. The light has come.

Scripture: Luke 24:1–12

Prayer: *Thank You, Father, for sending Your Son to be our Savior. Thank You for His mighty resurrection. Help me to know, in every area of my life, the power of His resurrection, so that my life may bear witness to this truth.*

Day 30

"**H**ow are you doing in science, son?" I asked, wondering if Joshua's knowledge of the subject was improving. It was the lowest grade on his sixth-grade report card in the second six weeks.

"I'm doing better, Dad," he replied. "Hey, guess what we are going to do next week—we are going to digest frogs."

I paused for a moment. He had mumbled a little.

"What did you say?" I asked, seeing a sermon illustration on the way.

"We are going to digest frogs," he said matter-of-factly.

"Don't you mean *dissect* frogs, son?"

"Yeah. Whatever," he said with a shrug of his shoulders.

"Joshua, *digest* means that you eat them."

"Yeah, I know."

I was never able to get permission to use this story when Josh was a boy. He finally granted me permission with the sagacity of a young adult. After all, when you're a kid, you say lots of dumb things, right?

And even when you are old you wish too often that you could gobble down words that jumped out when they should have remained in the boiling kettle inside. A child's error in vocabulary doesn't even require forgiveness—just understanding. But our errors with words are too often errors of the heart that reflect a bad attitude and a vengeful spirit. We do our warring with words, and we inflict much pain.

"Words can never hurt me," the old adage says, but it is wrong. Words can be knives in the heart.

It's a good reminder, this thing about words, when we are quarantined together in close quarters. Lots of words are being uttered in these trying times. We may be a little out of practice as conversationalists. We are wise to heed the counsel of Pastor James and keep our tongues in check.

Scripture: James 3:1–12

Prayer: *Guard my words today, Lord. Forgive me when they spill forth, and I know perfectly well what hurtful thing I am uttering. Give me self-control when it comes to my tongue so I can bless others with my spiritual presence in this world.*

Day 31

I woke up at 3:30 a.m., frightened by a dream I was having about a pandemic. Janet had already had such a dream.

I hate that this virus has infected my subconscious. Last night I discovered myself doing the breathing exercises someone recommended.

"They will not keep you from being infected, but they will help your lungs recover," they said. And there I was, lying in bed, taking deep breaths, releasing slowly, and doing it again. Protecting myself, I suppose, by getting a jump on the breathing machine.

I wore a homemade mask yesterday when I went to the store. It was made from a yellow bandana. It helped with the cold wind, and it reminded me not to touch my face. Maybe it won't stop all the droplets, like I read somewhere. But it does stop me from transferring anything from my hands to my face, and maybe it will protect someone else if I get infected.

The mask will likely be a psychological barrier to social interaction until its use is widespread in our community. It leaves everyone in the store guessing: Is the man sick, or does he think I am?

Talking itself may begin to fall under the label of "nonessential activity." It does require forcing air out of the lungs more robustly, and it often includes things like laughing and shouting. We may start talking less just to keep the breathing and the outbursts to a minimum.

"Keep it slow," I said to myself, walking down the aisle at the store, looking for mushroom soup. "No need to take a breath here. Too close to other humans. Wait till you get to the dairy section."

I couldn't hold it, though. There were too many brands of soup, and the regular-size cans of mushroom soup were sold out. I took a breath and grabbed the family size.

This dream—I can't remember the details. But if it reflects my disturbances then it must have included a foot-long cotton swab stuck up my nose and penetrating all the way to my brain. I always thought fondly of cotton swabs till now.

"As he thinketh in his heart, so is he," the ancient proverb goes (Proverbs 23:7 KJV). It's talking about me and my newly developed infection of the subconscious. A plague is more than a deadly microbe, I am realizing. It's also the preoccupation with sickness and death that an invisible bug casts like a net over the earth.

Scripture: Psalm 110

Prayer: *Dear God, today I want to find a thousand reasons to praise You. Fill my heart with Your presence. Help me to keep my balance spiritually and emotionally. May my words and deeds speak of complete confidence in You, even in the uncertainty of these days.*

Day 32

The sun came up like an orange ball over the eastern hills, and the wind had almost died. Birds sang in the oak trees. Sheep grazed in the pastures. One of my boat shoes, a gift from Joshua, was missing from the garage, carried off by Sadie the Golden Retriever, our grand-dog from New Orleans. I have wanted to impound her many times.

It was 37 degrees just before sunrise. Time for a fire.

My grandson Graham brought in a fistful of small sticks gathered from under the oak trees. We placed them in the fireplace next to the log that was partially burned from yesterday. We tore up the box that said "crunchy oats cereal." I found it at the grocery store, which did not have the brand of choice. I was the only one who ate any of it. Time to burn the box.

Graham must strike the match. It took him a hundred tries.

The heater came on just about the time the box got going, and all the smoke came out the front of the fireplace instead of going up the chimney. I closed the glass doors, and all the smoke boiled out of the crevasses in the doors and into the house.

"Someone must have closed the damper!" I shouted to Graham in a panic, stopping his effort to feed the fire with more crunchy oats packaging. I reached up above the fire and pushed the lever back, thinking it was wrong, which it was. The smoke got even worse. I pulled it back.

Nothing stopped the heater from sucking the smoke out of the fireplace. I turned off the heater and opened all the windows. The heater cycled too long, sucking that smoke into the house. Janet wanted it 69 degrees in the house when she got up. How about 39!

Most mornings are a mixture of blessings and crises, big and small. Life happens in a patchwork of smoke and sunshine.

We are collecting favorite verses to publish on the church Facebook page. One that was submitted came to mind this morning: "Finally, brothers and sisters, whatever is true, whatever is honorable, whatever is just, whatever is pure, whatever is lovely, whatever is commendable, if there is any excellence, if there is anything worthy of praise, think about these things" (Philippians 4:8).

Scripture: Philippians 4:1–8

Prayer: *God of smoke and light, teach me to view the world from Your divine perspective. Help me to focus my mind on what is good and beautiful. Keep me from becoming impatient and irritable when things don't go my way today.*

Day 33

"**P**apa, look!" Graham said, getting my attention this morning on the way to feed the animals. I turned to see him pointing toward the half-moon hanging above us. A bright orange sun was just about to peek over the plateaus to the east.

Everybody knows that humans are not responsible for the rising and setting of the moon and sun. Each episode of dawn and dusk is a gift to us. This knowledge has been around for thousands of years and is clearly stated in Hebrew poetry.

People of faith have insisted for generations that "the earth is the Lord's" (Psalm 24:1). This third planet from the sun, sailing and spinning through space, has an owner.

The Creator God called out to Moses from the burning bush. When Moses asked for his name, God said his name is *Yahweh* (Jehovah), the state-of-being verb, "I am who I am" (Exodus 3:14). (This name is translated as "Lord" and is in small caps in many translations of the Bible.)

People of faith have also insisted that people belong to God when they consider the rest of Psalm 24:1, "the world and those who dwell therein."

The One who brought us into being exists in a perfect state of being. He is all-sufficient, clothed in splendor and majesty, and the true ruler of this universe.

Times of uncertainty call us to trust in the One who brought us into being. We all agree that we are not responsible for the sunrise, that it is a gift to us. We do not control this universe or our solar system or the rhythms of this planet. All of these things are beyond our reach.

The world of science and medicine as we know it is now in a frantic search for a cure for a microscopic virus that threatens our way of life. We all hope and pray that we will find an antidote. When we do, we will celebrate worldwide the conquering of this microbe that brings such trouble to us.

Somewhere in all of this there is a lesson in humility for all who expect to conquer the earth.

Scripture: Psalm 24

Prayer: *Creator God, You are exalted above the earth. Your majesty covers the heavens. I ask for Your help in these trying times. Give me the perspective of heaven. Help me point others to You!*

Day 34

Jesus spoke spiritual truths through parables. The word *parable* has "para" in it, like parallel. The preposition is often a part of Greek words, like *paraclete,* "one who comes alongside," a comforter.

Parables lay down a story beside our lives to help us understand what is going on in us and in our world. It is a general term in Greek for figurative speech: "The kingdom of heaven is like . . ."

Jesus told Nicodemus, "The wind blows where it wishes, and you hear its sound, but you do not know where it comes from or where it goes. So it is with everyone who is born under the Spirit" (John 3:8).

I set up the RV next to the house recently. I am using it now as an office. Grandchildren are great, but it helps sometimes to have a little social distance.

The RV has a large mechanical awning that I extended out to provide shade on the eastern side. But I could hear the wind whipping it as I worked, and I decided to retract it.

The wind is like the Spirit, Jesus said. *Wind* and *spirit* are the exact same Greek word.

The wind is powerful. So is the Spirit of God.

The wind is mysterious. So is the Spirit of God.

The wind reveals it presence without revealing its origin. The same is true for the Spirit.

The wind makes noise but does not tell where it is going.

The wind does what it pleases without instructions from us. The same goes for the Spirit of God.

If you listen, you will hear the Spirit of God at work in your world. You will see His activity around you. I hope your eyes and ears are open to His presence. You cannot join the Spirit of God in His work unless you know what He is doing.

The work of the Spirit around you is not something you initiate. He initiates His work, including the call to join Him.

Scripture: John 3:1–16

Prayer: *Father, give me eyes to see Your activity in my world and in the people about me. Give me courage and faith to know how to join You in the work You are doing. Give me patience in prayer to keep seeking until I am able to see.*

Day 35

How did a primitive Polynesian culture move stone statues weighing forty-five tons each several miles from the quarry where they were carved to their resting place on treeless Easter Island?

Early theorists suspected the gods came down to assist in the project. More recently some assumed UFOs brought visitors from outer space who moved the 324 massive figures. More than a thousand statues were carved, but most were never moved.

Scientists now theorize that in AD 400 Easter Island was covered with a dense forest full of game and wildlife and supporting a population of some four thousand people. The project to carve and move the statues began, and trees were felled by the thousands as tools for the task, including rollers and supports.

A thousand years passed, and the forests were completely depleted, along with the wildlife that was a major source of food. The inhabitants turned upon one another, and the population quickly fell to about 170 people.

The deforestation of the island remained a mystery because in the intervening centuries all indications of Easter Island's previous woodlands were erased.

Our personal resources, both physical and spiritual, are limited and will only be sufficient through the weeks and months and years ahead if we are replacing what we are expending—if we are planting as well as harvesting.

These days of difficulty make great demands on many people. Those of you who are medical professionals may be working long hours caring for the sick. You also experience anxiety about catching COVID-19 and the possibility of infecting your loved ones. You may worry about the possibility of going into quarantine when you are needed at home and work.

Some of you are caring for children, trying to homeschool for the first time in your life. Your additional responsibilities may also increase the daily stress.

If you are carrying an extra load during these days of the coronavirus, then you are using extra resources of courage, stamina, determination, patience, and commitment. You are chopping down some trees.

How are you holding up under this load? Are you running out of inner resources? Have you found a way to renew your strength? Isaiah 40:31 says, "They who wait for the Lord shall renew their strength; they shall mount up with wings like eagles."

Do not turn your life into a barren Easter Island. When the project or the challenge is particularly costly, always take time to replant, to receive God's renewing within. Build into your daily schedule some minutes to meditate and pray. Plan to take off a couple of days and get away from the weight of it all.

Taking time for renewal of internal resources will help with confusion, irritability, anger, and despair. God rested on the seventh day, not because He was tired but because humans get tired and need some time off every week.

Scripture: Isaiah 40:27–31

Prayer: *God of grace and power, help me to be a good steward of my inner resources, emotional and spiritual. Help me take time today to wait upon You and enjoy the renewal of my inner strength.*

Day 36

"Papa," my grandson Brady said as he turned toward the garage. "Can you get the caterpillars off my bike?"

We had decided to make a trip to the mailbox, and he wanted to ride the bike. He was barefoot, and his boots were in the garage.

I never before heard a request like that one, but then, I never saw so many caterpillars. They rain down outside our door like one of the plagues in Egypt. The six oak trees in my yard must be hosting six million of them, hatched and looking for food.

Some of these caterpillars are harmless. But some have spines up and down their bodies. If you step on them—or they fall down your shirt—you are about to experience some pain.

Brady had one fall down his collar yesterday as he was walking around outside. He rubbed that spot, not knowing what it was. He must have squished the caterpillar and spread the poison because he developed a caterpillar-size burn on his neck.

Isolation and quarantine do not mean the absence of temptation to sin. In fact, sometimes a relaxed schedule and routine make us susceptible to emotions and actions we would previously have avoided.

The Apostle Paul wrote to the church at Ephesus. He told them to "Get rid of all bitterness, rage, anger, harsh words, and slander, as well as all types of evil behavior" (Ephesians 4:31 NLT). In other words, get rid of all the poisonous caterpillars crawling on your bicycle.

We've been in close quarters in our homes for more than a month now. We are all experiencing the anxieties of the plague. Our routines and relationships are disrupted. The future remains uncertain. Our retirement nest eggs go up and down like giant waves in the ocean.

Anger and harsh words may germinate and spread under such circumstances. We may retreat into old habits that we know are unproductive and even destructive.

Let's not go there. Let's identify the spiny crawlers and get rid of them before they do their damage to us.

Scripture: Ephesians 4:22–32

Prayer: *Father in heaven, I thank You for the gift of this day and of Your presence in it. I pray that You will protect me from the temptations that surround me. May the pressures and stresses of this day bring out the best in me, not the worst.*

Day 37

Dealing with teenagers during stay-at-home orders? Things may not be as different as they seem. This encounter with my then-teenage children was thirty years ago:

Rachel reached to turn on the television. "No," I said. "It is late, and you have had enough TV."

"But Dad—"

"No 'buts,' Rachel. Go to bed."

"It's vacation time, Dad," she pleaded, beginning to grovel.

I looked at her sternly. She formed the word "please" with her lips and leaned her head to one side.

"Go to bed—immediately after you finish the movie." She punched the on button as I disappeared down the hall.

My ears were smitten by raucous chords from a birthday jam box. I marched into Rebekah's bedroom and punched the stop button. She sat Indian style in the middle of her bed with a book cradled in her legs. She looked up, startled by the silence. "Dad!" she cried in horror. "That's Carman! It's a Christian tape!"

"Go to bed, Rebekah."

I whirled on my heel and left the bedroom. As I passed Joshua's room, I happened to catch him turning on his fan.

"It is too cold, Joshua," I said, and snapped off the fan.

"Dad," he said, "I like snuggling up in the covers. I can't sleep without the fan going. The noise makes me sleepy."

"Good night, son," I said with a sigh, snapping the fan back on and turning out the light as I left.

I thought about the three encounters with my children. Realizing that I had been inconsistent, I made another trip down the hall, charged into Rebekah's room, and turned on her music.

What's wrong with me? I wondered, and the answer seemed to be—*your kids are growing up.*

Could it be that your most recent parental dilemmas are products of their age rather than your own? The moral dilemma of "who decides" is not so pressing when they are preschoolers.

Scripture: Colossians 3:18—4:6

Prayer: *Give me wisdom, Father, as I relate to my family. Teach me the balance between law and grace. Help me to grow in my walk with You as I struggle in my changing role among those I love so much.*

Day 38

I remember my own father's pilgrimage from the stern disciplinarian of my early childhood to the more benevolent approach of later years. Both my parents changed. The toddler who was their charge twenty-seven years after I passed through the ranks did not receive exactly the same treatment I did (It's true. I do have a brother twenty-seven years younger than I). Parents get older, too, and less energetic.

The desire to establish a Christian home is stronger than ever, but the essentials may not be what I once thought they were. My mother grabbed one of my little brothers one day and covered him with kisses. I was married then, I think, but still without children. I told my mother, "You are going to spoil him."

She said, "David, you cannot love them too much."

The heart of the home is love. The heart of friendship is love. The heart of the church is love. The heart of God is love.

I trust that my love will be a love with standards and guidelines and positive discipline. I pray that my love will be shaped by the Word of God, by the character of Christ. I do not want a spineless love or a nebulous love.

But I do want love to be the flag of the family, the emblem of the house, the coat-of-arms. I do not expect that emotion is the heart of my love. I expect that daily instruction and timely chastisement are closer to being its best indicators.

I have been amused and amazed at the change that comes over parents when they become grandparents. The sternest of dads is a pushover as a granddad. What is going on?

In part it is the shift of responsibility; in part it is the passing of years. Somewhere in between the doting grandfather and the dreadful dad there is a perfect mix of menace and mercy.

You learn the best lessons just after you need them.

Scripture: Psalm 136:10–26

Prayer: *Help me, Lord, to know You better today because You are the perfect blend of love and holiness. Forgive me when I fail to act with the proper balance of these two beautiful qualities. Keep me on Your anvil, shaping me more perfectly into the image of Your Son.*

Day 39

Packages of cocaine with a street value of half a billion dollars were found at the Napoleon Street Wharf in New Orleans in the fall of 1998, hidden inside a metal transformer case. The lab in Colombia that manufactured those packages had its stamp on the wrappings.

The police burned it all because it is a deadly and illegal poison. The market for it was so great, however, that other shipments were sneaked into the country successfully and ended up on the streets.

In a world warped by addiction and desperation, demand for the white powder is measured in billions of dollars. Jails and prisons brim over with those convicted of drug-related offenses. Humans become enslaved by their passions and desires. We have not learned yet how to avoid the things that kill us and embrace the things that give life.

Counselors and physicians warn that this season of quarantine and social distancing will cause an increase in addictive behaviors, including alcohol and drug abuse. These substances may be legally purchased and even prescribed by a physician. Even so, they can be abused and become destructive.

A wild man, driven by demons, knelt at Jesus' feet and found sanity, wholeness, and freedom from his bondage. The light of Christ continues to bring that same liberty in our day to people with all kinds of addictions.

We all have our temptations. If we are not careful and prayerful, these days of unusual stress and isolation will weaken our defenses and cause us to fall back into behaviors that we know are deadly to our health and our relationships.

Whatever the chains that bind you, Jesus is the name of your freedom. Keep your Bible open. Find your comfort and peace in God's Word and presence in your life. Stay connected to the people who really love you.

Scripture: Luke 8:26–39

Prayer: *Lord Jesus, protect my mind and heart and health during this time of stress and isolation. Be with those who are troubled by addictions. Deliver them from the deadly poisons. Give our physicians, counselors, and church staff wisdom as they seek to help those who are struggling. Thank You that your power is stronger than any addiction.*

Day 40

My daughter Rachel was preparing for a college exam one morning many years ago over breakfast. This was during the time when she was a psychology major. She switched majors half a dozen times, I think.

"Ask me some questions," she said, handing me a notebook with scribbled handwritten notes. For the next forty-five minutes I questioned her about abnormal psychology. I learned about depression, diagnostic and treatment paradigms, unipolar and bipolar abnormalities.

About ten minutes after seven she said she had to go get dressed. I assumed she was already dressed for school, silly me. Five minutes later she was on her way to Waco. Just like her dad, I thought. Gave herself about fifteen seconds' leeway to get to class on time. No wonder she holds the world's record for Baylor University parking tickets.

I learned that morning that some people get stuck in adolescent or childhood developmental phases, which may be illustrated by little graphs with squiggly lines. When I saw these graphs, I knew that I, at least, was abnormal.

I also learned that morning that there are weather-related and holiday-related dips in the emotional graph. There may even be weekday-related dips. Some of you saw the cartoon—I think it was Calvin and Hobbes—that graphed the five-day work week. The poor guy started out at the bottom and gradually recovered until by Friday he looked like he was going to live.

How does your pandemic graph look? Is it following the curve of confirmed cases? Is it tracking the Dow Jones? Yikes!

We live in a time of worldwide upheaval. I prayed last night for friends, relatives, and church members who are sick with COVID-19. Whether you or your loved ones have the virus or not, it has invaded your prayers and changed your life.

My friend, you are going to live. Whatever the dip in your emotional status, "this too shall pass." Most things get better by morning. And even if they don't, you know how the last page reads, and we win. We who know Christ as Lord should never lose hope no matter how the squiggly lines are going.

Scripture: 2 Corinthians 4:1–12

Prayer: *Keep me looking up, Lord, especially when I feel the weight of the world on my shoulders. Let me live in hope today, knowing that my strength comes from You. Thank You that You are equal to every task I must face this day.*

Day 41

I talked to a young man who went through an eschatology stage. He read books on the mark of the beast and the Battle of Armageddon. He watched CNN and read the newspaper, looking for the signs of the times.

He got confused and afraid. The process began to paralyze him spiritually and emotionally. He abandoned that focus, he told me, and now just wants to know more about Jesus.

Jesus has a powerful sense of the end (*telos*) in His preaching. His words contain many warnings about being ready for the end of the age. He came preaching the coming of the kingdom of God, that the kingdom is *among* us through His presence and that it is *coming* in a future glorious revelation and consummation.

Jesus lived His life, I believe, with an eye to the end of the age. He had a long view, a hope anchored in the future work of God, which shaped his life and behavior.

He stockpiled no weapons, however, and He engaged no government authorities in battle. He did not retreat to a mountain to live with His followers, as some of His contemporaries did, nor did He withdraw to the desert to await the climactic judgment.

Instead His expectation of the coming kingdom of God supported the practical realities in his life—love of the Father and love of His neighbor.

That is how it should be in our lives as well. COVID-19 is spawning many mental and emotional storms. As with all crises, some people interpret this plague as a sign of the end of the age and the wrapping up of all things.

It could be true. Jesus could come at any moment. But if He comes now, we want to make sure we are doing what He commanded us to do. When He comes, we want Him to find us busy doing what He commanded. We want to be found sharing the gospel, loving our neighbor, and doing unto others as we would have them do unto us.

Scripture: Mark 13:32–37

Prayer: *Keep me working, Lord, as I watch for Your coming. Do not let me slide into slothfulness or grow weary on my watch. Help me to act today in such a way that, should You come, I would be pleased and not embarrassed.*

Day 42

The visitor center at the mouth of Carlsbad Caverns has a fascinating video that plays over and over. It features a park ranger narrating the saga of the cave night life.

"These are the Mexican freetail bats," the ranger says. "The colony peaked in population many years ago at about two million. Now it stands at about 250,000 and appears to have stabilized there." The voice continues as the little screen shows thousands of bats flying out of a gaping hole until they blacken the evening sky by sheer numbers.

"Almost all of these are female bats. They come here to Carlsbad to have their young." The cameraman has taken pictures of the little bats hanging with their mothers upside down on the roof of the cave.

"After five or six weeks the young bats have grown old enough to attempt their first flights," says the narrator.

Now that statement caught my attention. I thought about the desperate situation of those little bats. The narrator says, "They have no second chance." The voice crackles in the speakers overhead. "They must make their first flight in total darkness, navigating instinctively by using their sonar faculties. Many do not succeed."

Did you freeze at the end of the high dive on your first attempt? We have all witnessed that inner struggle at the swimming pool as a newbie climbs up the ladder, walks out the board, takes a look, turns around, and climbs down.

So what failure do you fear most today? God waits to have that fear given unto Him so He can replace it with faith and trust. He calls us to rest in His love, to enjoy His peace. He is not looking for our inner turmoil but for the attitude of heart that places all things at his feet.

Scripture: Hebrews 11:1–6

Prayer: *Help me, divine teacher, to live in faith, not fear. Free me from the paralysis that comes when I fear I will fail. Show me how to recover when I have fallen, and help me to embrace the truth that no failure is truly final.*

Day 43

As I write this devotion, we have streamed our worship services and Sunday school classes for seven Sundays and have not gathered in the building. We are approaching the number of Sundays we were exiled from the church facility in New Orleans after Hurricane Katrina—eleven. Our congregation was scattered all over the country then, made refugees by the great storm and terrible flood.

Church is very much about one another. We love each other as Jesus loved us. This is His new commandment to us. We do this by caring for each other. We often express our love and care face to face.

Now we express our love and care from a distance. We love each other as much as we ever did, and we miss each other. But knowing how contagious this virus is, we distance ourselves from one another as a way of showing love and care.

We have practiced social distancing for years whenever infections required it. We understand better than any previous generation the science of communicable diseases. This is part of the reason we enjoy greater health and longer life, on average, than previous generations.

But we have not practiced social distancing to this extent in our lifetimes. This is a unique experience for us in our society and, especially, in our churches. We are not familiar with this lifestyle, but we are familiar with the principle behind it.

Religious liberty and the right to assemble are enshrined in the Bill of Rights. The First Amendment to our constitution guarantees us these liberties. Houses of worship receive special treatment because they deal with matters of conscience and faith.

Science, however, is the same for a church as it is for any other organization. This is the reason we construct church buildings in compliance with building codes. It's the reason we comply with government regulations in food service, fire codes, occupancy certificates, and many other aspects of our work.

I miss our gatherings terribly, but I do not feel that my religious liberty has been infringed upon. Rather, I feel that our government is doing its job, trying to keep us all safe, and that our civil authorities have a compelling interest in mandating social distancing for all groups, including churches.

Paul wrote to the church at Corinth: "Even though I am not physically present, I am with you in spirit" (1 Corinthians 5:3 NIV). He was referring to a bond of love that makes us one in Christ and overcomes all the distance between us.

Scripture: Psalm 121

Prayer: *Dear God, thank You for Your strong arm and Your comforting presence during these strange days. Give me the inner strength I need to be a support to my friends and family. Help me show my love and concern for others even when we cannot see each other face to face.*

Day 44

Imagine a little bat curled up comfortably beside its mother. It is warm and well-fed. It enjoys life. Everything it needs is provided. Then the mother speaks:

"Son, it is time to make your first flight." The bat has never seen her, although it is familiar with her sound and smell. It has no idea, as a little bat, that it hangs upside down one hundred feet above a solid rock floor. It lives in a cave so vast that, should it get lost, chances are high that it will never be found.

The mother nudges the little bat, encouraging it to test its wings. She calls upon it to release the grip it has always had upon the rock ceiling and, falling through space, activate the sonar skills it has never used in flight. It must use its wings in flight for the first time. It must use these skills well enough to avoid diving into the hanging stalactites and scattered stalagmites. And it must be able, after successful flight, to return to its mother's side in a colony of 250,000 bats. All of this must be accomplished in total darkness.

When it attempts its first flight, it will not be the only little bat diving into the perpetual night. Hundreds of other novice navigators will attempt their first flights, dashing this way and that, some thudding against the walls of the cave, others losing their way, never to return.

The world has no bravery to compare with the courage of month-old bats. The bat ought to be featured along with the lion, the tiger, the bear, and the eagle.

As fate would have it, however, the bat has neither the beauty nor the stature to impress the masses. Its bravery generally remains in secret. I suspect this may be the case with most genuine bravery. Genuine courage is the bravery that moves the heart to do what is necessary despite the fear, the unknown, and the terrible possibilities.

Scripture: 2 Kings 7:3–11

Prayer: *Lord, I see courage when I see You in Your trial and crucifixion. Would You develop such courage in me? I am too often afraid. Give me courage today to face whatever comes, knowing that Your grace is sufficient for every challenge.*

Day 45

My father told his teenage boys that the guardian angels would fall off the car hood if we traveled too fast or turned too sharply as we were driving. I learned to drive with this image of an angel perched on my right front fender.

The interest in angels in our generation parallels an equal interest in the Middle Ages when theologians actually debated how many angels could dance on the head of a pin. It also parallels a great interest in the first and second centuries when angelology (the study of angels) reached a peak.

There are 143 references to angels in the New Testament and 83 references in the Old Testament. Some of these are actual appearances of angels. Others are teachings that involve angels, such as Jesus when He says the angels will separate the good from the bad at the end of the age. (See Matthew 13:47–50.)

Most of the references to angels in the New Testament occur in Matthew, Luke, Acts, and Revelation.

The Christmas story involves angels more than any other part of the Bible except Revelation. Angels visited with our Lord Jesus on a couple of occasions and appeared at the empty tomb after His resurrection. The Book of Acts records a number of angelic visitations that protected and guided the early church.

Angels are part of the created order. They are given authority over creation and history in the Bible. They are specifically assigned to protect children, protect God's people, watch over the activities of nations, and carry out the judgments of God.

The term *angel* literally means "messenger." God's people have been comforted throughout the ages by the knowledge that God's angels watch over them, just as the Bible teaches. Psalm 91:11–12 (NIV) says, "For he will command his angels concerning you to guard you in all your ways; they will lift you up in their hands, so that you will not strike your foot against a stone." This is particularly true in times of great trouble and crisis, such as the world is experiencing in this pandemic.

Scripture: Hebrews 1:1–14

Prayer: *Father in heaven, thank You that Your angels camp around us to watch over us. Thank You for the protection You give us every day, from dangers known and unknown. Keep me in Your care today as I seek to live for You.*

Day 46

The storm woke me up about 3 a.m. with lightning flashing through the window curtains. Then the thunder started to rumble.

I got up, pulled on a shirt and pants in the strobes of light, and hunted for the flashlight. The wind was picking up, and the rain had begun to pepper down. I opened the back door and watched the storm. I checked to see if the small coop was still upright, which it was. It has fifteen little chicks inside.

I opened the side door. The golden retriever was noiseless in the garage. She has been known to howl and whine during storms.

The front door gave me another angle. Hail mixed with rain had begun to ping down on the sidewalk and porches, some of it marble-size.

I was watching the hail skip around when a snake made the corner at the front of the house and headed toward the front door where I was standing. It slithered along on the wet sidewalk right along the foundation, under the eave where there was some protection from the hail.

The snake moved slowly toward the door where I stood. The flashlight beam seemed not to deter it. I opened the door and spoke to it. Still it came on.

It was three feet long at least, a beautiful patchwork of smooth browns, blacks, and tans with a pointed tail. No rattler.

I got the broom from the washroom and swept the snake six feet away from the door in one stroke. Once it recovered, it headed toward the door again, seeking shelter in the storm.

The rain and hail stopped, but not the snake. I thought about the boys playing around the house and decided I'd better send the snake to the afterlife and discard his remains in the floodwaters still running through the culvert under the highway.

These snakes—they're like the weeds in the parable of Jesus. Just when you think you have your two acres tamed, one of them shows up to occupy your space. I guess that's what happened in the Garden at the beginning. Adam and Eve thought they had the orchard claimed from the wild, and then the wild got in them. This can happen to you, you know, during the isolation and disruption of shelter-in-place. Just when you think your life is in order, the snake appears to curl up on your doorstep. You know what I'm talking about.

Scripture: Genesis 3

Prayer: *Protect me, Lord, from the notion that I have conquered all my temptations and fears. Keep me real about my own weaknesses and vulnerabilities. I need You, Lord, I need You. Every hour I need You.*

Day 47

We heard an enormous racket the first night we had our cat at the new house in the country. The cat insisted on going outside, and when the door was open, he made a beeline away from the house and refused to be captured. I chased him across the field until he disappeared into the grass along the creek. Janet loved that cat.

When the noise erupted, we thought at first that Josh had come home and turned the television on full blast. I got up and checked. Josh was not home, and the television was not on.

We did not see our cat after that terrible noise. The neighbor confirmed that a band of coyotes was roaming the area and that several pets had fallen victim in the night.

I rehearsed my attempt to catch LeBeau. He simply would not cooperate. I guess he wanted to explore his new world, unaware of the danger he was in when separated from us.

Humans have this roaming spirit in them as well. We all feel the longing to explore the edges, the periphery, the perimeter. We are challenged by our peers and by our own inner yearnings to go beyond the limits. We are gifted with curiosity. We want to see what is beyond the next turn in the road.

We can venture safely into new territory only when we are with our Shepherd. He is our protection. If we insist on going where He forbids us to go, then we leave behind our protection and move from courage to folly.

Jesus commands us to stay connected to Him. How can you stay connected today? You must begin and continue in prayer, continually aware that He is with you. Times of pain and trouble offer open doors of opportunity for the words and deeds of the gospel.

Jesus lived a life full of adventure, and so will you, if you follow Him. As you go about your day you will discover all kinds of places where God is working. You can join Him in that work.

Scripture: John 15:1–9

Prayer: *Master, I long to exercise faith, but I do not want to be foolish. Show me the difference between these two. If You are with me, I am willing to go anywhere. Without You, Lord, I dare not even draw another breath.*

Day 48

As I write this I have finished up six weeks of safer-at-home recommendations, and they have flown by for Janet and me as we have hosted Brady and Graham, our two youngest grandchildren. We have ground a track into the yard around the house riding our lawn tractor and ATVs. If we had to move three steps, we cranked them up. We have fed chickens and sheep to our hearts' content and gathered eggs at least once a day.

The boys' mother insists on taking them home to New Orleans today. She has work to do, and their dad is waiting to see them too. I get that, but I still wish they would stay a little while longer.

As we think about a grand reopening of life as normal, it is also a great opportunity to rethink and reconfigure. It includes making decisions about changes that need to be made. The need for these changes may be long-standing. Even better. We all have an open door of opportunity to adjust our lives for better outcomes.

I have heard a number of people talk about their spiritual disciplines during these days. Some have renewed their prayer life and found great strength and peace. Some have returned to reading the Word of God daily. Some have decided to reconnect with their churches by attending online Bible study and worship.

The quarantine experience may have reminded you of a season in your life when you were more faithful in the things that really matter.

You can jump right back into your previous schedule and behaviors.

Or you could rethink and retool with the goal of improving your inner life, your character, and your relationships. You could get reacquainted with the people you are supposed to love and reconnected to the God who made you for Himself.

Scripture: Genesis 32:22–28

Prayer: *Dear Lord, I know You love me and want to bless me. I pray that You will give me wisdom and courage as I restart my life and activities. Show me the adjustments I can make that will bless my friends and family. Help me to stay close to You.*

Day 49

Reopen with Jesus in your mind and heart.

A lot of meanness goes on in the world. People return evil with evil. A slap on the cheek will explode in a fight. Hating your enemy is common human behavior.

Jesus of Nazareth challenged this propensity toward violence and conflict in us. He told us to return evil with good, to bless those who curse us. He taught us to turn the other cheek and go the second mile. He taught us to love our enemies.

These are simple ideas, but they are not easy. Many Christians have never really accepted them as a true guide for their behavior.

We who follow Jesus have the Holy Spirit within us. The Spirit of God is present to inform our decisions and guide our thoughts. We are supposed to be committed to acting in ways that are loving and just, not hateful and cruel.

We apply these teachings at the personal level, although they go against our old nature. But it is harder to see how they apply at the social and corporate level.

Too often our institutional goals seem devoid of conscience. In business and industry, we who follow Jesus cannot afford to define our purpose simply in terms of materialism. We must put conscience into all of our goals and purposes whether we are plumbers, bankers, retailers, or shop foremen.

We develop a "community" conscience by elevating the importance of people. We can be focused upon the needs of people whether we are in business, industry, education, or government. And we can be focused on the needs of people and the value of people regardless of where we are in the pecking order of our institutions.

We are all refurbishing, rethinking, and reopening. Let's define our purpose with the words of Jesus. Let's seek to meet the needs of people. Seek to foster justice and love among people in our institutions or professions. Apathy, dishonesty, and selfishness seem to be throttling our culture. A return to brother-keeping as part of our institutional agendas will inspire our people and help stem the social chaos.

Scripture: Isaiah 5:18–25

Prayer: *I want to be faithful to You in my business, Father. Show me how to build structures that are just. Help me be responsible to my brother in the workplace. Give me courage and creativity to be an advocate for justice and truth and mercy in all the circles of my life.*

Day 50

My younger brother, Tom, and I were reminiscing and remembered suddenly a motorcycle race we had when we were young adults. The family owned two pretty powerful motorcycles at the time, mostly used for tearing around in the pasture and jumping terraces.

Tom and I got out on the paved road and were caught up in a race for just a few minutes. We were traveling close together at about eighty miles per hour when—*splat*—we hit a swarm of bees.

Going that fast, you slam through a swarm of bees in a split second. When we stopped the bikes, we found that we were covered with bee juice. Little red welts appeared all over our exposed skin—not stings, but welts from the impact with the bees. How many of you can say you slaughtered a hundred bees with your body and were never stung?

Had I known that swarm was coming, I might have hit the ditch at eighty miles an hour, and who knows what would have been the outcome. But I didn't know it. I didn't see the swarm coming, and I road safely through it.

I told Janet one day, "I wish I knew what was coming." And she said, "No, you don't." I thought about it for a moment and had to agree with her. Our security is not in our knowledge. If we knew, we might swerve to avoid the bees only to end up wrapped around a tree trunk. Jesus knew what was coming as He prayed in the garden of Gethsemane, and He required all His spiritual resources to take the cup His father gave Him. We would be overwhelmed had we been in His place.

The prophet Isaiah said "When you pass through the waters, I will be with you; and when you pass through the rivers, they will not sweep over you" (Isaiah 43:2 NIV). And we might add, "When you hit the unexpected bee swarm, I will carry you through unstung."

Scripture: Isaiah 43:1–13

Prayer: *I trust You with the future, Lord, for You know the future better than I can know the past. I believe You are in control even when I am helpless to change things myself. Give me the peace that comes from childlike faith, and help me live this day resting in You and unafraid of tomorrow.*

Day 51

The chicks are afraid of grass. The blades move in the breeze, I guess. They will not jump off the down ramp from the hutch.

They are ten days old now, eating a lot of medicated starter mash and drinking lots of water. They fly around in their little house thumping into things. They would enjoy the greater space and the dirt—chickens love dirt. But not yet.

Strange sounds, unexplained motion, unfamiliar shapes—these things are cause for concern. Do they pose a danger? We are not certain. We hesitate, contemplating, suspicious, then go back to the familiar.

Some scholars think the word *Hebrew* is derived from a verb that means "to cross over." Abraham was called a Hebrew by the residents of the Land of Canaan because he crossed over the Euphrates River. The Euphrates was one of the great borders in that part of the world.

Abraham believed God. He followed the voice of God as he left his homeland. Acting by faith, he left "not knowing where he was going" (Hebrews 11:8).

God speaks to people about new activities, new relationships, and new directions for their lives. In order to follow God, we will have to leave behind familiar patterns and lifestyles. We will need to trust Him as we follow His voice and undertake the new things He calls us to do.

Crossing over a familiar boundary and entering a new territory is both exciting and fearsome. how you become one who crosses over.

Abraham and his descendants had this reputation for facing their fears and attempting new things. They defied Pharaoh and left the slavery of the land of Egypt. They crossed over the Red Sea. They conquered the Promised Land. They gave birth to a new reality as they listened to God's voice and followed Him.

I sprinkled some of their food on the down ramp and a little on the ground. The chicks loaded the ramp. It took two minutes for one of them to touch the ground.

Scripture: Hebrews 11:1–10

Prayer: *Dear God, give me more faith. Help me to trust You more fully. Keep me from acting in fear as I reopen my life and emerge from this stay-at-home season. Give me boldness to believe You and to follow Your prompting in my heart.*

Day 52

Working as a pastor in Gatesville, Texas, has reconnected me to an important season of my life. I served for six years as pastor of Trinity Baptist Church here in Gatesville, and I was a volunteer in the prison system during those years.

I remember sitting on the concrete floor just outside of Karla Faye Tucker's cell on death row. She was new to prison and a new believer in Christ. I brought my guitar, and Pam Perillo, Linda Burnet, and Karla would join me in singing songs of faith. Often our chorus would drown out the curses and shouts from the inmates on the psychiatric ward.

Karla came to know Christ in the Houston jail partly through the instruction of a Baptist chaplain. I had the privilege of instructing Karla weekly in the way of Christ when she was new as a believer.

Karla was a true believer, a magnificent witness to the power and grace of God. No one who knew her doubted the authenticity of her faith. Guards and fellow inmates alike developed a great love and respect for her as a godly woman. She was a transformed individual, one of God's trophies of grace.

She was executed for her crimes by lethal injection in Huntsville, Texas, in February of 1998.

Pray today for the person who seems to be a lost cause, that person you have prayed for many times before with no visible results, that person you have seldom prayed for because you thought down deep inside it would do no good.

Pray for the seven thousand inmates in five prisons in Gatesville as they struggle with anxiety about illness. Pray that those who know Christ will be bold in their witness during this pandemic. Pray that others will see their need for the Savior. Pray for the employees who interact with them every day.

One thing I learned for sure as I saw Karla grow into a dynamic witness for Christ—there are no dead ends in God's grace!

Scripture: John 8:1–11

Prayer: *Thank You, God, that Your grace is greater than all our sin, that no one is too great a sinner to be saved. Bless the prisoners. Help them to walk in faith if they know You. And help those who do not know You to find You as Savior and Lord.*

Day 53

My mother called her cousin Betty yesterday. She lives in a nursing facility in New Jersey. Mom was concerned because she had heard from a sister that Betty, who is 88, the same age as my mom, had contracted COVID-19.

Betty answered her phone. She had recovered from the virus. Mom was looking forward to a long conversation with her cousin. Their families were close when they were girls— camping trips, revival meetings, overnight stays. They had lots to talk about.

Except that Betty couldn't hear a thing unless Mom shouted. Mom is getting a little hard of hearing herself, though I haven't told her, but Betty was approaching stone deaf.

Mom enjoyed her call with Betty, she said, but "my ears rang all day from the shouting." It was too bad, she said. She'd like to talk to her cousin again, but the shouting was just too unpleasant.

"She's nearly blind as well," Mom told me, and I could see her shaking her head in dismay. "I don't think I'll call again."

The afflictions of the coronavirus do not diminish the regular challenges of old age. They add to them.

Mom is from vigorous German ancestry. Her great-grandmother, Christina Weiler, turned one year old while on the ship that brought her family to America in 1832. She gave birth to my great-grandfather, George Earnest Riethmiller, in Pennsylvania. There have been several centenarians in the family. I hope Mom will be one of them.

Longevity is usually a blessing, though I recall with pause the regular prayer request of Mrs. Edwards. She was bedridden and wanted to die and told me to pray for her death at each visit. She lived ten more years in her miserable condition and died at age 107.

Long life inevitably includes many difficulties, no matter who you are. My mother was born in 1932 during the depths of the Great Depression. Her childhood memories include the unusual social circumstances of World War II.

I am grateful for God's promise: "Even to your old age and gray hairs I am he, I am he who will sustain you. I have made you and I will carry you; I will sustain you and I will rescue you. . . . 'My purpose will stand, and I will do all that I please'" (Isaiah 46:4, 10).

Scripture: Isaiah 46:1–13

Prayer: *Sustain me, Lord, during these days of difficulty. Hold me up with Your hands. Encircle my life and my loved ones with Your strong arms. I am trusting in You today.*

Day 54

Some Sunday nights we had seven volleyball teams competing at Center City Baptist Church between Star and Goldthwaite. One of the youth, Willie, won a calf-roping contest when he was a senior in high school, but he couldn't keep the money because that would make him a professional athlete. Willie gave the money to the church. We bought sacks of concrete and poured a basketball court one Saturday, all of us working together. We mounted the lights on two long lengths of pipe and welded the basketball goals.

You wouldn't call it pretty. The concrete was rough enough that you didn't want to fall down, and it wore out the basketballs. John, Willie's dad, was built like a Hereford bull and played basketball like one too. Getting on his side was the safest move you could make, especially on that court. Barbed wire fences on two sides only sometimes stopped the balls that misfired, and wandering outside of the circle of light at night could get you into prickly pear or other pasture hazards.

People came from as far away as Pottsville, Mullin, Moline, and Goldthwaite to play ball with us on Sunday nights. When we had too many people for the recreational facilities, the ones waiting to play or just watching would sit in metal folding chairs under the live oak trees and sing with the accompaniment of guitars, mandolins, and harmonicas. Thinking back now, I realize we were practicing social distancing, outside and scattered.

I married one of the young ladies who trusted Christ during that time, and my first staff position in a church was serving there as youth director.

Isn't it amazing how God uses such different settings to accomplish his work? Have no doubt. He is at work around you even when your circumstances seem strange and confusing.

We have experienced strange and confusing in spades these last two months, but look carefully and you will see the hand of God.

Scripture: Proverbs 3:1–12

Prayer: *Show me what You are doing in my family and my place of work. Give me eyes of faith so I can see Your hand. Help me be sensitive to those around me. Increase my courage, Lord, so I can speak about Christ to those who are seeking answers.*

Day 55

John Burris was the one who started my interest in the guitar. He would bring his beat-up guitar, a mandolin, and three or four harmonicas. He had a neck mount for the harmonicas so he could strum and blow at the same time. All of his fingers were thicker than my thumbs. I don't know how he managed to press down just one string at a time. He would sit in a folding chair in a grassy spot near the live oak trees. All of us would pull up chairs and benches from the church and watch him keep time with a big, booted foot. Sometimes he'd wear his cowboy hat setting way back on his head.

I learned to play his guitar first and then got one of my own. Before long I was sitting on my bed at home with a guitar in my lap writing songs about Jesus and singing them at church. I wrote one called "Mighty Hands." Thinking about it now, I wonder if John's hands weren't part of the inspiration. My friend Willie bought a size 15 senior ring, and John couldn't put it on his little finger. I saw him displaying that monster ring, and it was jammed on his smallest pinky, right at the base of the fingernail.

Those massive hands could calm a frightened mare, toss a lariat, or bulldog a steer. We were hauling hay one day and found a big nest of yellow jackets hanging from the roof of the barn. I asked John what we should do since it was right in the way. John climbed on the stacked bales up to the nest, took aim, and squashed the whole thing with one hand. I'm telling you the truth. He had to swat one or two that got away, but he mashed the rest and never got stung.

I guess I have fingerprints all over my life from people who left their impressions, especially when I was young. You are leaving fingerprints today. Even small hands with slender fingers leave deep impressions. Do a good job.

Scripture: Proverbs 4:1–27

Prayer: *Watch over my words today, Lord. Help me speak words of hope, healing, and love. Keep me from exploding with anger or speaking foolish words that damage my witness for You. Help me be especially careful with the most impressionable people in my life. Let me act in love alone.*

Day 56

I left my collection of novels from Moody Press at Center City in the Baptist church. The Baptist church is right next to the Methodist church. Janet and I were married in the Baptist church and then walked over to the Methodist church for our reception.

That collection of two dozen novels by Christian authors helped shape my teenage years. I figured at the time, being sixteen, that maybe some other youth could benefit from them. The stories were all about growing up and how to act like a Christian, but they were full of adventure and romance too, which made the reading interesting. I bought them through a book club, the kind that keep sending you books and bills even after you cancel three times. I couldn't really afford to belong to a book club, working turkeys being my only source of income, but I paid the bills and read the books.

Our family included five teenagers at the time we moved to Center City. The youth department really took a big jump. The church fathers decided to tear out a wall when our room was too full, but they never patched the plaster where the wall used to be. I could still see that seam last time I stopped by to look in the church.

I also saw my novels, still sitting in the same little book-shelf I'd placed them in when I was a boy decades ago. I don't think anyone ever read those books. The lizards and bugs used them for cover when people came through.

The books served a great spiritual purpose in my life. It's okay if they fell into disuse after that. Many things are seasonal, including things that sustain us in times of crisis like this COVID-19 era. The Creator God intervenes in our lives through people, circumstances, and His Word in ways that are unique to the season we are in. New support emerges, and former things dim. Only God is changeless.

Scripture: Deuteronomy 6:1–9

Prayer: *Father in heaven, you have provided for me from the time I was born. You have watched over me and brought me to this day. Thank You for Your tender care through so many relationships and circumstances. May I be happy and useful in Your kingdom today.*

Day 57

Today as I write this devotion, it is Mother's Day, so naturally I'm inclined to read Proverbs 31. The virtuous woman described in this passage is involved in business and commerce. All she does is accomplished in the context of her family. She is a homemaker of enormous energy, ambition, and devotion. She is not domesticated, but she is domestic. She is not greedy, but she is astute. She is not complacent, but she is content.

This woman is clothed with strength (v. 25). Strength is something she puts on every day. She is determined to be strong for her family and for herself. True strength of character is not in the genes but in the will. The wise choose strength over weakness.

She is also clothed with dignity. She has a sense of herself that is not arrogant but is confident. "She laughs at the time to come" (v. 25). Honesty and courage and hard work have given her an air, an aura, that straighten the back, quicken the step, and hold the head high. She knows the importance of her work and her ways, and she is purposeful in all she does.

The family rallies around this wife of noble character. The children respect her and bless her, and her husband praises her. She has made the safety and provision of her household the consistent priority, and that decision now blesses her on every hand. She worked to establish such a family through the years, and now she enjoys the fruit of that labor. She wears the dignity of a job well done.

This woman is fearless, and she fears the Lord. Other qualities, like charm and beauty, are fleeting. But godly virtue endures as the true choice of the wise.

Scripture Reading: Proverbs 31

Prayer: *Dear Lord, thank You for my family and friends. Help me to be faithful to the ones You have given me to love. Give me strength every day to choose what is right and good. Give me the dignity that comes with hard work, wise choices, and deep faith.*

Day 58

God gives us wisdom to know what we can change and what we must accept as unchanging. I cannot change my shoe size. I must simply accept that. There are many such things we must accept and receive. Other things, like my weight or my heart rate, I can work to change. And I ought to take appropriate actions where these are concerned.

When living under adverse conditions, make sure to practice gratitude. Paul says, "Give thanks in all circumstances; for this is the will of God in Christ Jesus for you" (1 Thessalonians 5:18). The little word *in* is important here. We do not need to give thanks *for* all circumstances, but we can give thanks *in* all circumstances.

If the fog has rolled in, you can be grateful for past sunny days or the coming spring. You can be grateful for the time by the fireplace reading a book. You can be grateful that the soccer game was canceled because the field is too wet.

Sometimes when conditions are difficult in our lives, we really do not have normal visibility. Our vision is shortened by the looming, overpowering nature of the adverse situation. That grief or sickness or disaster or pandemic that has come into our lives will loom smaller as time goes by, and we will be able to see better.

It is best in the meantime to drive a little slower, to treat ourselves gently, and not to rush into new and unfamiliar settings. God is at work in these current circumstances, troublesome though they may be. He will use them in your life for His glory. Trust in Him.

Scripture: 1 Thessalonians 5:12–24

Prayer: *Today, Father, I want to live with a grateful heart. Give me gratitude that flavors every thought and flows out with every word. Use my difficulties for Your glory.*

Day 59

I walked to the pond one afternoon, just thinking and enjoying the outdoors. As I approached, I saw two small forms walking along the water. They paused when they spied me, staying frozen in their positions until I got close enough to see them. They were odd-looking birds with long legs and black bills, about the size of a seagull or smaller, and seemed to be from the same general family of birds. When startled, they took to flight.

I walked around the pond to where they sat for so long watching me, and they made a pass by me, calling in a strange, clipped bird song that may have been intended to frighten me. I got curious and began to survey the ground around me. I found racoon tracks but no evidence of a nest. I proceeded around the rest of the pond, looking for anything that resembled a nest and found it twenty steps away. It was a hole in the mud. They had burrowed down about four inches, piled the mud around the hole, and twisted a few strands of grass and weeds into the mud. There were no eggs.

Could this be a nest, right here? I wondered. The pond was six feet lower than normal. Any run off would cover and destroy the nest. It seemed terribly exposed to wild creatures, especially racoons that frequent the pond, or snakes that love eggs. And it was going to flood at the first good rain.

Not only the nests of mud hens, but also many other nests are vulnerable to predators and the elements, including human homes. We must be wise to build our homes with ample protection for the young. They are most vulnerable and depend upon our vigilance.

The pandemic is disrupting many nests that were intended to be safe and secure. Tempers flare as stress, anxiety, and fear have their way in our lockdown.

Godly character is the best protection we have from the troubles at home. Relationships so intimate require peace, self-control, patience, and, most of all, love. These are the fruit of the Spirit. They manifest themselves as we trust God in the trouble.

Scripture: Psalm 91:1–16

Prayer: *Protect our children, Lord, for they are most vulnerable in the twisting currents of life. Give us wisdom to know their needs and courage to set the rules. Help us act always in love for them. We commit the children to You in faith, Heavenly Father.*

Day 60

A newborn calf scrambles through a fence and ends up on the road. Newborn dragonflies, still immobilized by the trauma of metamorphosis, make good eating for birds and amphibians. Snakes love bird eggs, and fish eggs are a delicacy for almost everything in the water.

The latest newborn lamb struggled to his feet amid the rocks and the cacti, his eyes still partially glued shut. The sun was hot at midday, and his mother nuzzled him this way and that until he collapsed in a little shade under the paddles of a prickly pear. I wasn't sure he would make it, this wobbly little life, but he was galloping and skipping in just a day or two.

It is a time of vulnerability for all living things, this cycle of nest-building and procreation—including humans. No family is more vulnerable than when the nest is just being built and the little ones are still just toddlers.

I went over to the day care at my church one morning and said hello to a gymnasium swarming with tiny creatures. When they saw me, several of them sped up on tricycles or ambled over with the swagger of a crawler just turned walker. They tried to talk to me, but I did not understand their language. One of the little ones pressed up to my leg and laid her head on my knee. I don't know who she was.

They are so trusting when they are one or two. You can win them to friendship with just a quiet word or song or simple hug. They cannot discern between good and evil motives then. They have little fear of strangers. That must be ingrained in them later on by world-wise adults.

God entrusts the little ones to parents (and grandparents and other caregivers) who are stronger and wiser. During those first vulnerable years, our presence is required so that

129

they may develop spiritual and moral sensibilities, be protected from predators, and learn the art of human community.

Scripture: Proverbs 1:8–19

Prayer: *Help the children grow in their knowledge of You during these days of stay-at-home. Bless the parents and other adults who stand in for teachers and help with online school. Help our churches as we reopen the children's ministries. Keep us all safe. Give us ample helpers and a growing love for the little ones.*

If you enjoyed this book, will you consider sharing the message with others?

Let us know your thoughts at info@ironstreammedia.com.

You can also let the author know by visiting or sharing a photo of the cover on our social media pages or leaving a review at a retailer's site. All of it helps us get the message out!
Facebook.com/IronStreamMedia

———————

Iron Stream Books, New Hope® Publishers, Ascender Books, and New Hope Kidz are imprints of Iron Stream Media, which derives its name from Proverbs 27:17, "As iron sharpens iron, so one person sharpens another." This sharpening describes the process of discipleship, one to another. With this in mind, Iron Stream Media provides a variety of solutions for churches, ministry leaders, and nonprofits ranging from in-depth Bible study curriculum and Christian book publishing to custom publishing and consultative services.

Through our popular Life Bible Study, Student Life Bible Study brands, and New Hope imprints, ISM provides web-based full-year and short-term Bible study teaching plans as well as printed devotionals, Bibles, and discipleship curriculum.

For more information on ISM and Iron Stream Books, please visit IronStreamMedia.com